Roman

and

Oklahoman

A Centennial History
of the
Archdiocese of Oklahoma City

James D. White

Publisher
Éditions du Signe
B.P. 94
67038 Strasbourg cedex 2
France
Tél: 011 33 3 88 78 91 91
Fax: 011 33 3 88 78 91 99
Email: info@editionsdusigne.fr

Publishing Director
Christian Riehl

Director of Publication
Joëlle Bernhard

Publishing Assistant
Audrey Gilger

Design and Layout
Daniel Muller - M@W

Photography
John Glover

Maps
Paul Tourigny

Photoengraving
Éditions du Signe - 105220

ISBN 2-7468-0750-5

Printed in China by C&C Offset Printing Co., Ltd

Archbishop's Greeting

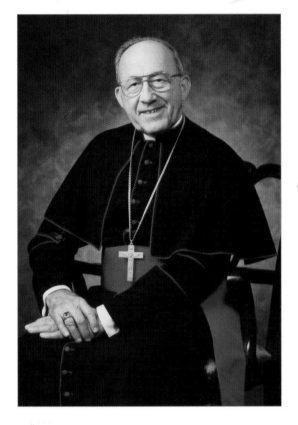

My dear Brothers and Sisters in Christ:

JESUS directed His disciples to go into the whole world and proclaim the Good News. For two thousand years, men and women of faith have joyfully responded to this invitation. The Catholic Church, established by Jesus Christ, is faithfully fulfilling His command.

The formal presence of the Catholic Church in Oklahoma began in 1876 with the appointment of Father Isidore Robot, OSB, as Apostolic Prefect of the Indian Territory. On April 20, 1891, Bishop Theophilus Meerschaert was appointed the new Apostolic Vicar. On August 17, 1905, Pope Saint Pius X established the Diocese of Oklahoma. The growth of the Church throughout the Twentieth Century led to the creation of the Diocese of Tulsa and the elevation of Oklahoma City to a Metropolitan See on December 13, 1972.

On August 17, 2005, the Catholic Church of Oklahoma will celebrate the one hundredth anniversary of the establishment of the Diocese of Oklahoma. With great faith and joy and optimism, this jubilee book, expertly prepared by Reverend James D. White, commemorates this centennial event.

As a former Bishop of the Diocese of Tulsa and currently the Archbishop of Oklahoma City, I gladly present this book as a tribute to those who went before us in faith. May it also serve as a challenge for us today and as a sign of hope for the Catholic Church in Oklahoma in the future. All this is because Jesus assured us when He said: "I am with you always, even to the end of time." (Matthew 28:20)

Sincerely yours in Christ,

+ Eusebius J. Beltran

Most Reverend Eusebius J. Beltran
Archbishop of Oklahoma City

Author's Preface

IN 1997, as the Archdiocese prepared to observe its twenty-fifth anniversary, work began on a comprehensive history of the Church in central and western Oklahoma. Each parish, along with many of the institutions which have been part of Catholic life in Oklahoma City and other urban centers, was asked to prepare a history. Although a considerable amount of material was gathered, the project bogged down and was left uncompleted. Now, as the centennial of the Oklahoma diocese approaches, another effort has been made to assemble the earlier material, bring it up to date, and publish it as a celebration of the one hundredth year since the Diocese of Oklahoma was established on August 17, 1905.

I have adopted an approach to this history that may seem unorthodox by today's standards. Even though Oklahoma has often been described as a missionary diocese, and even though it was at first named for the Indian Territory, the fact is that its parishes have mainly developed in response to white settlement that followed the successive land openings —nine of them in all— that began in 1889. Consequently, I have organized the parish histories according to their locations within the territories, in the order in which those territories were opened. While this may seem confusing, I think that it gives a good overview of the very real relationship between the history of the Catholic Church in western and central Oklahoma and the societal development of those regions of the state. (Two indexes, one on page 48 and the other on page 142, will be helpful in locating the individual parishes and missions, as well as churches which have closed.)

The 1997 project, ambitious as it was, was but the latest in a long series of historical accounts of the Oklahoma Church that go back well into the the nineteenth century, beginning with the journals of the Benedictine Fathers who arrived here in 1875. Their first publication, *The Indian Advocate*, which debuted in 1890 and ran continuously for twenty years, is still an important source for the researcher. Likewise, *The Orphans' Record*, published monthly from St. Joseph's Orphanage west of Oklahoma City between 1913 and 1921, was important for its historical surveys and for being the precursor of the diocesan newspaper.

In addition, the work of academic historians such as Father Joseph F. Murphy, O.S.B., Sister Mary Ursula Thomas, O.S.B., Sister Alicia Middeke, R.S.M., Sister Mary Louis George, O.S.B., and Thomas Elton Brown have provided a wealth of information about our early Church; and gifted amateurs such as Bishop Theophile Meerschaert, Bishop Francis Clement Kelley, Father Urban deHasque, Joseph Quinn, Father David Monahan, and Sister Martha Mary McGaw, C.S.J., have made major contributions toward preserving the large and small details of our common life in the Faith. A special word of thanks to Jeanne Devlin, Patrick McGuigan, and Father Thomas Boyer, who assembled and coordinated much of the research that went into this volume. They have every right to claim equal authorship of this newest history of the Oklahoma Church.

I am grateful as well to Carol Davito, Brother George Hubl, O.S.B., and Joëlle Bernhard and Audrey Gilger, of Éditions du Signe, in France. My particular thanks to Cara Koenig, of the staff of *The Sooner Catholic*, for her intensive work in collecting and arranging the photographs for this book.

Skiatook, Oklahoma
May 23, 2004

This stained-glass window is from the Cathedral of Our Lady of Perpetual Help, Oklahoma City.

Table of Contents

1 The Beginnings

around 1541

✧ There was a time when not even shrubs such as these grew on the plains of western Oklahoma.

A T the start, there was nothing. Or as near nothing as anyone could imagine. The land lay as empty waste, a long downhill slide from the Rockies to the Mississpi. Its streams were wide, shallow, and usually empty, and its surface was a chaotic sea of tall grass that caused vertigo in anyone unlucky enough to stumble into it.

For centuries it was just there, the dried bed of a prehistoric inland sea that had formed from melting glaciers and had once stretched all across the middle United States. The first inhabitants, the Wichitas from the north and the Comanches from the south, were nomads who began settling here around the end of the 1400's, just when Europeans were learning that the earth was far larger than they had supposed.

The Coronado expedition probably crossed through western Oklahoma in 1541, and it certainly returned through the Panhandle in 1542. Numbering about a thousand soldiers, priests, and camp followers, the group marched into western Kansas, where it found potential converts but no other riches. When the disappointed Spaniards returned to Mexico, one of

the priests, a Franciscan named Juan de Padilla, remained behind with the Wichita tribe; but they misunderstood his intentions and killed him in November 1542. He thus became the first martyr of the North American mainland.

The Spanish lost control of Oklahoma to the French in 1682, then regained it in 1763, as political struggles in Europe impacted events in faraway places. Spain, by now heavily invested in Texas and the territories

✧ By the last half of the 19th century, the once proud Plains Indian tribes had been reduced to hardscrabble poverty.

Oklahoma: The Twin Territories

In 1834 the term Indian Territory began to be used for the region set up as a receiving ground for the native tribes already being cleared from the area east of the Mississippi River. It consisted of all the land between the great river and the Rocky Mountains, except for places that were already (or would later become) states or territories.

By 1870 this huge area had been reduced, approximately, to present-day Oklahoma. From about 1825 to 1866 the Indian Territory was the domain chiefly of the Cherokees, Creeks, Choctaws, Chickasaws, and Seminoles. After the Civil War, however, some 60 other tribes, most of them already uprooted more than once, were relocated here. The tribes were issued homelands that were generally on the borders of the Indian Territory itself. This left some 1,800,000 acres in the middle—the Unassigned Lands.

Pressure had been building for years to open these lands to white settlement. In the spring of 1889, Congress finally passed the necessary legislation, and President Benjamin Harrison set noon on the day after Easter—Monday, April 22— as the opening hour. An unexpected 50,000 persons, from as far away as Europe and Australia, showed up for what became the Land Rush, and by nightfall there were six new towns and 9,000 homesteads on the empty plains.

The next year, 1890, Congress passed the Organic Act, which provided a political infrastructure for this new region, the Oklahoma Territory. Over the next sixteen years, this Territory grew, as tribes were persuaded to forfeit legal title to the lands they held by treaty. Successive openings, of different types, occurred in 1891, 1892, 1893, 1895, 1901, 1904, and 1906. At last, on November 16, 1907, President Theodore Roosevelt signed the Enabling Act. The Oklahoma and Indian Territories were joined as one, and Oklahoma became the 46th state.

---

farther south, could not spare administrators for the Central Plains, so they simply employed the French officials who had been seeing to affairs in the vast region.

One of these was an officer named Athanase de Mezieres, whose headquarters was in Nacodoches. Around 1778 he rode out to where two Wichita villages faced each other across the Red River. These he developed into the commercial posts of San Bernardo and San Teodoro. San Bernardo was in what is now Jefferson County, south of Ryan. San Teodoro, a smaller settlement, was located in present-day Montague County, Texas. A third Wichita village, northeast of Newkirk in Kay County, was likewise designated a trading post around the same time; it became known as Ferdinandina.

At a council of the Catholic bishops of America in 1833, pastoral care of the vast region west of the Mississippi was entrusted to a band of Jesuits, numbering about a dozen and headquartered near St. Louis, Missouri. One of these, Father Charles Van Quickenborne, while seeking contact with a part of the Osage tribe, was in northeastern Oklahoma as early as 1830. After

1850, missionary priests based in Kansas, Texas, and especially Ft. Smith, Arkansas, made short forays into what by then was being called the Indian Territory. The first priests to settle permanently, however, were two French Benedictine monks, refugees from the aftermath of the Franco-Prussian War, who arrived in Oklahoma in 1875 by way of Louisiana.

They were Father Isidore Robot, O.S.B., (1837-1887) and his companion, Brother Dominic Lambert, O.S.B. (1838-1915). Delegated by their abbot to find a congenial home for the about-to-be-exiled community in America, and encouraged by a visit from the archbishop of New Orleans, Napoléon Perché, they showed up on the archbishop's door in 1872. That worthy man, who had not realized he was setting in motion such a chain of events, assigned them to live as chaplains at a convent of the Sisters of Mercy in Shreveport. But he did not forget them. He got in touch with one of his suffragan bishops, Edward Fitzgerald of Little Rock, who had

✧ By sheer coincidence, two of the handful of early Benedictines were named Isidore. This is Father Isidore Ricklin, O.S.B., the dynamic founder of St. Patrick's Mission at Anadarko.

✧ By 1896 Sacred Heart had grown to include a two-story monastery, with a large abbatial church *(center)* and St. Mary's Academy *(at far left)*.

a problem of his own. Besides the whole state of Arkansas, he was responsible for pastoral care in what maps of the time referred to as Western Arkansas, that is, the Indian Territory. Since he had only six priests at his command, this was obviously too heavy a charge.

(Actually, it was not clear at the time exactly who did have jurisdiction over Catholic Oklahomans. The Little Rock diocese dated from 1843, but in 1851 Rome created something called the "Apostolic Vicariate of the Indian Territory east of the Rocky Mountains"— in Latin, *vicariatus apostolicus territorii Indorum orientem Saxorum montium*—an amorphous region encompassing at least modern Nebraska, Kansas, and Colorado, and having its headquarters on the Potowatomi reservation in Kansas. It eventually became the archdiocese of Kansas City, Kansas.)

(The Jesuit assigned to the vicariate, Bishop Jean Baptiste Miége, assumed, not without reason, that he was responsible as well for the Indian Territory south of Kansas; thus Jesuits from Osage Mission, Kansas, regularly visited McAlester, Ft. Sill, Ft. Supply, and points between until 1885. Not until 1883, in response to a direct question about the matter, did Rome decree, somewhat after the fact, that Little Rock had had the prior claim.)

At any rate, Fitzgerald and Perché were eager to devolve the Indian Territory into someone else's responsibility, and Isidore Robot, who seems to have been chiefly interested in locating his Benedictine brethren in a place free from civil and ecclesiastical oversight, was happy to become the first resident priest in Oklahoma. Fully aware that the Roman legal mills were now grinding away, he and Dominic Lambert left Ft. Smith in October 1875. They had been inclined to settle among the Osages in the area around Pawhuska, but the Osages failed to answer their letter of inquiry, so they went instead to Atoka, in the Choctaw Nation, where stood the sole Catholic church in the Indian Territory. It was the work of Irish railroad men building the Katy line through eastern Oklahoma into Texas.

From Atoka Robot and Lambert made an initial tour of the whole region, eventually deciding that as hosts the Potawatomi were a better bet than either the Choctaw

or the Osages. The Citizen Band Potawatomi who, like the other portions of the tribe, had been evangelized earlier by French Jesuits, offered the monks one square mile of land in exchange for a church and school.

In September 1876 the documents arrived from Rome informing Robot that he was now the apostolic prefect of the Indian Territory, the chief Catholic missionary priest to the region. (The difference between a prefecture and a vicariate, by the way, is that a prefecture is generally entrusted to a religious order, one of whose priests serves as the prefect, while a vicariate is governed by a bishop.)

It thus came about that Sacred Heart Mission was founded in a couple of log cabins near the south end of the Citizen Potawatomi Nation in May 1877. Within three years Robot, with financing from mission-minded Catholics in France and New York, would build a large monastery, separate schools for boys and girls, a vocational-technical school, and the beginnings of a seminary. It would be several years before his interests extended to building any parish structures.

✧ This tiny chapel, St. Patrick's in Atoka, was the sole evidence of Catholicism in Oklahoma when the first Benedictines arrived in 1875. It had been built three years earlier by Irish railroad workers.

The First Priests

THE first missionaries to settle permanently in Oklahoma were Benedictine monks from the Abbey of Ste. Marie de la Pierre-qui-Vire in France. The first two, Father Isidore Robot and Brother Dominic Lambert, arrived in the Indian Territory in October 1875. After other monks had arrived, Sacred Heart Mission was founded in the Potawatomi Nation, growing to become Sacred Heart Abbey and then—relocated 35 miles north to Shawnee—St. Gregory's Abbey. Over time the first monks were joined by others—French, Basque, Italian, Belgian, and American— some of whom remained in Oklahoma, while the rest left for other houses of the Order.

Bishop Meerschaert, who came in 1891, set about recruiting priests and seminarians from Europe, especially from his native Belgium and the neighboring Netherlands. Between 1893 and 1924, some 46 Dutch and Belgian priests came to Oklahoma.

Between the Benedictines and the Belgians, from 1886 to around 1895, there were five other diocesan priests with service in Oklahoma. Their backgrounds are shadowy, and it is even possible that one of them was an impostor.

Father Frank Rouquier is said to have been from Canada. He appeared in Oklahoma in 1886 and was assigned to Purcell, where he built the first church. He left the next year, but returned briefly in 1888. In 1890 he was on the Quapaw reservation in northeast Indian Territory. Nothing more is known of him.

For years it was thought that Father Nicholas Francis Scallan (N.F. Scallan) was from Australia, but we now know that he was born in Iowa of Irish parents, was ordained for the Dubuque diocese, and later went west to work in the missions of the Dakota and Idaho territories. He was in Arizona, at Mission San Xavier del Bac outside Tucson, when the 1889 Land Run occurred. Within two

✦ Father N. F. Scallan.

weeks he had arrived in Oklahoma City, and he said the first Sunday Mass there on May 5. He helped to start parishes in Edmond, Oklahoma City, and Norman. He was born with a rare genetic disorder called albinism, which affects the formation of skin pigment. Albino humans have pinkish-white skin, white hair, and pinkish-blue eyes. They are adversely affected by bright light and hot weather. Father Scallan left Oklahoma around July 1890, went to Salt Lake City, Utah, and died there on October 15, 1892. He is buried on the grounds of New Melleray Abbey near Dubuque.

Father Joseph Beck was born around 1839 in Switzerland. He arrived in Oklahoma in 1889. From 1891 to 1897 he was active at Kingfisher and at Hennessey, where he built the first churches. Bishop Meerschaert dismissed him because of alcoholism. He died in Nebraska in 1914.

Father George Theodule Dugal was born in Montreal, Canada, in 1844. He served in the Holy Cross order, then in several dioceses, including that of Leavenworth, Kansas, (now the Archdiocese of Kansas City, Kansas). Apparently he was dismissed from there, came to Oklahoma in 1891, and served briefly in the Osage Nation. From around 1895 to 1902 he was an oblate in residence at Sacred Heart Abbey. He died on January 13, 1902, and is buried at Sacred Heart.

Father Arthur Gustave Borremans, born in Ghent, Belgium, arrived in 1892; the first mention of him is at Guthrie, where he was an assistant pastor in December of that year. Nothing is known of his movements before then. He was the first priest to say Mass in Perry following the Run of 1893. In 1894 he was appointed to Kingfisher and Okarche. He was transferred to Ponca City in 1897, had some personal problems there, and left the Territory in 1900.

Cradle of Catholicism

✦ Sacred Heart in its glory days, around 1900.

SACRED HEART, on present-day State Highway 9, in the southeast corner of Pottawatomie County, is among the historic treasures of Oklahoma. Founded in 1877, it was a rare center of civilization on the Indian Territory frontier. Benedictine officials in Rome named it a priory in 1892 and an abbey in 1896.

Several schools, from elementary grades through theological seminary level, flourished here. Jim Thorpe attended first grade at Sacred Heart, and all manner of travelers, from priests to outlaws, received hospitality from the monks. It even had its own U.S. post office, with Father Isidore Robot, O.S.B., as the first postmaster. The Sisters of Mercy had their first Oklahoma foundation here in 1884. It was also the headquarters of the apostolic prefecture of the Indian Territory; the fledgling Oklahoma church was governed from Sacred Heart until 1891.

It all came to an end on the night of January 15, 1901, when the entire campus of frame structures was consumed by fire. Students returned to their homes, and the monks scattered to various places in the U.S. and elsewhere. One large building was rebuilt, but by this time it had become obvious that no railroad was going to come anywhere near Sacred Heart, and so the schools could never draw pupils from any distance.

Fortunately, the town fathers of Shawnee had the idea of offering free land to groups that would build colleges there. The result was Oklahoma Baptist University on one side of Highway 3 and St. Gregory's College on the other. The Catholic University of Oklahoma, as it was called at first, opened its doors in September 1915. Soon it was a matter of the tail wagging the dog, as the foundation at Shawnee outstripped the nominal headquarters at Sacred Heart. Finally the abbatial seat was transferred in 1929, and the Shawnee institution became St. Gregory's Abbey, with Sacred Heart once again a simple priory. The cradle of Oklahoma Catholicism finally shut down for good in 1954. A few outbuildings and cemeteries for the early monks and the Sisters of Mercy remain, along with the Sacred Heart parish church.

2 Prefecture

July 5, 1876 - May 29, 1891

WHEN the Roman missionary department (technically, it was the Congregation for the Propagation of the Faith) created the apostolic prefecture of the Indian Territory, it appears to have been the first prefecture established in what was at the time a United States territorial possession. (Alaska, created in 1894, was the only other one.) Dom Isidore Robot found financial support from a lay-based organization in Lyons, France, the Society for the Propagation of the Faith, and from a Catholic newspaperman in New York named James McMaster, who adopted Robot and his mission as a personal project.

McMaster's motives were mixed. On the one hand, he sincerely admired Robot and his vast task in the wilderness, but he was equally driven by his dislike for a man named Charles Ewing. The archbishop of Baltimore had put Ewing, a layman, in charge of an agency called the Bureau of Catholic Indian Missions. Ewing was the brother-in-law of General William Tecumseh Sherman, and had himself held the rank of general during the Civil War, while McMaster, although a Northerner, had been a Confederate sympathizer whom Ewing had caused to be interned for the course of the war. By supporting Robot, who had his own problems with Ewing's bureau, McMaster was thumbing his nose at Ewing.

Meanwhile, pressure from the expanding white population of the United States had been driving many Native American tribes west of the Mississippi, where they were assigned homes in the Indian Territory. 67 tribes, or remnants of them, were settled in the region. They came in two waves. The first began around 1825, and involved tribes mostly from the Eastern seaboard of the United States. The second started after the Civil War, especially during the 1870's, as the U.S. Army battled the Plains Indians who were resisting America's westward expansion.

Significant white settlement began on April 22, 1889, when some 50,000 home seekers poured onto 1,800,000 acres that had not yet been assigned to any tribe. Other land runs followed as the government maneuvered, first to reduce the size of the reservations, and then to extinguish tribal title altogether. Oklahoma would become the 20th century's first newly-admitted state on November 16, 1907.

❖ In an early example of acculturated liturgy, Father Urban de Hasque (second from left) and Father Isidore Ricklin, O.S.B. (right) watch as Kiowa medicine men prepare cedar smoke for a purification ceremony.

❖ Father Willem Huffer at an Indian home on the treeless plains, probably around 1920.

❖ Middle picture: The Pioneer Woman statue in Ponca City.

Catholic Tribes

✧ A grove of trees offers shade as Father William Ketcham (far right) preaches the Gospel to a congregation of whites and Quapaws in the early 1890's.

ODAY about 35 Native American tribes are represented among the citizens of Oklahoma. Each tribe has its own particular history, and one should not draw general conclusions about Native Americans as a group from the lives and customs of any single tribe. Catholic efforts at evangelizing Indians west of the Mississippi were limited to the Jesuits of the Mississippi Valley and the far Northwest, and the Franciscans of the Southwest. In general, the Plains tribes that later were located in Oklahoma did not benefit from Catholic missionizing. Native American Catholics in the Archdiocese of Oklahoma City either originated east of the Mississippi, as did the Citizen Potawatomi Nation, or else they were evangelized after they came to Oklahoma by Benedictine monks from Sacred Heart Mission.

Citizen Potawatomi Nation

Traditional history records that the Potawatomi, Chippewa, and Ottawa peoples were a single tribe living on the northern shores of Lake Huron. By 1700 the Potawatomi had moved southward and located near modern Chicago, Illinois, where they were first evangelized by French missionaries from Canada. By the Treaty of Chicago in 1833 the tribe ceded about 5,000,000 acres of land to the United States. By 1840 most of the Potawatomi were living west of the Mississippi. The tribe had always lacked unity of action, and it split into numerous bands. One of these, the Citizen Band, was settled first in Kansas, where St. Mary's College would later stand. In 1867 the Citizen Potawatomi Nation moved to what is today Pottawatomie County, Oklahoma. Ten years later the nation granted a square mile of land to French Benedictine monks for a monastery and school. This became the precursor of St. Gregory's Abbey and University at Shawnee.

Tribes of the Anadarko Agency

The federal Indian agency at Anadarko was established in 1869. It was intended originally for the Wichitas, but gradually came also to serve the Caddos, Kiowas, Comanches, Apaches of Oklahoma (formerly the Kiowa–Apaches), the Fort Sill Apaches (Chiricahuas and Mescaleros), and the Delawares. All seven of these tribes were influenced to some extent by St. Patrick's Mission School, also at Anadarko, though it cannot be said that any of them adopted Catholicism as their tribal religion. By the time Catholic missionary activity began among them, around 1875, too much had happened to these groups for them to adopt a united tribal vision of God or Christianity. By this time religion, for the Indians, was becoming a matter of individual choice rather than a component of native culture, even as it already was with Anglo-Americans.

Prefecture to Archdiocese

JULY 5, 1876

Pope Blessed Pius IX decreed the existence of an entity called the Apostolic Prefecture of the Indian Territory. A prefecture is a first step toward organizing the Church in a mission area. In 1876 there was but a single priest in what is now the State of Oklahoma.

FATHER ISIDORE ROBOT, O.S.B.

The priest's name was Father Isidore Robot, O.S.B., from the Abbey of Ste. Marie de la Pierre-qui-Vire southeast of Paris. The prefecture was entrusted to the Benedictine Congregation of the Primitive Observance, the part of the order to which the French abbey belonged. Father Isidore was given the title of prefect. He was never more than a simple missionary monk, even though in 1879 Pope Leo XIII bestowed on him the honorary title of abbot. He is best known for founding Sacred Heart Mission, which would eventually become Sacred Heart Abbey, and then St. Gregory's Abbey.

FATHER IGNATIUS JEAN, O.S.B.

Father Isidore died in 1887, shortly after a successor arrived in the Indian Territory. This was Father Ignatius Jean, O.S.B. He remained only a little more than two years, but they were eventful ones. Several new missions were started as a result of the interest shown by millionaire heiress Catherine Drexel and her two sisters. The first Land Run was held in April 1889, and Father Ignatius preached to the waiting settlers the previous day —Easter Sunday— in Purcell. And there were high-level discussions about changing the governance of the Church in the Territory.

MAY 29, 1891

BISHOP THEOPHILE MEERSCHAERT

In April 1891 Father Theophile Meerschaert, vicar general and rector of the cathedral in Natchez, Mississippi, learned that he had been selected as the first (and as it turned out, the only) Apostolic Vicar of the Indian Territory. A vicariate is different from a diocese because there is no cathedral and no chancery. It is assumed the bishop/vicar will spend most of his time in the saddle as a roving missionary. Meerschaert was consecrated in Natchez on September 8 and arrived in Guthrie on the 19th, to begin 32 years on the job.

AUGUST 17, 1905

It took fourteen years to bring the Territory to the next step. In August 1905 Pope St. Pius X signed the decree creating the Diocese of Oklahoma. Bishop Meerschaert moved his headquarters from Guthrie to Oklahoma City, took possession of St. Joseph's Cathedral, and appointed his first chancery officials.

NOVEMBER 14, 1930

Because of the growth of Tulsa as a center of Catholic activity, Bishop Kelley asked the Holy See to change the name of the diocese to that of the Diocese of Oklahoma City and Tulsa. One effect was that the cathedral was moved from St. Joseph's in Oklahoma City to Our Lady of Perpetual Help. In addition, Holy Family Church in Tulsa was designated a co-cathedral.

FEBRUARY 6, 1973

The final step was announced on December 17, 1972: Oklahoma City was to be an archdiocese, Tulsa was to become a separate diocese, and these two, along with the Diocese of Little Rock, would form a new ecclesiastical province, the Province of Oklahoma City. The ceremonies confirming this were carried out in Oklahoma City on February 6, 1973.

3 Vicariate

May 29, 1891 - August 17, 1905

AMONG those who flocked to this last frontier were a small number of Catholics. They did not declare themselves as such to the authorities, and so we do not know their names. No ethnic group predominated among them, although small pockets of Italians, Poles, Germans, and Czechs developed over time. In 1891 the entire Catholic population of Oklahoma was generously estimated at 5,000, or about two percent of the total.

That year the Benedictine prefecture was elevated to the rank of a vicariate, and a Belgian diocesan priest working in Mississippi, Theophile Meerschaert, was named bishop and apostolic vicar of the Indian Territory. His assigned residence was Guthrie, capital of the Oklahoma Territory—the area newly-populated by white homesteaders.

Bishop Meerschaert faced three main challenges—in personnel, finances, and in the sheer physical distances he had to travel. He recruited priests and begged money in his homeland, but he did not do much to encourage vocations in Oklahoma. Only one Native American was ordained in his lifetime, and the first two white Oklahoma-born diocesans were not ordained until 1928, four years after his death. As to distance, in 1894 a pastoral visit to a single mission at the western tip of the Oklahoma Panhandle involved a round-trip of 1600 miles by train and buckboard through Kansas, Colorado, and the New Mexico Territory.

Although the evangelizing of Native Americans was a nominal priority, the lack of missionary manpower, uncertainty as to aims and methods, and the cultural disorientation of the tribes themselves resulted in few lasting conversions. A sizable chain of Indian mission schools was begun by the Benedictines and carried on under Meerschaert. Most of these were funded by Mother Mary Katharine Drexel, a major benefactor of the Oklahoma Church, through the Bureau of Catholic Indian Missions. Enrollments at the schools were small—never more than a hundred—and by 1930 most of them had closed or were taken over by adjacent white parishes.

Oil exploration in Oklahoma began on the Osage reservation in 1896. Until then, Pennsylvania had been home to the oil industry, and many Pennsylvania oilmen who came to Oklahoma were Catholics, chiefly of Irish heritage. Because of the wealth which oil brought to its developers, the Catholic population of Oklahoma would tend to have political influence in the state that was disproportionate to its numbers.

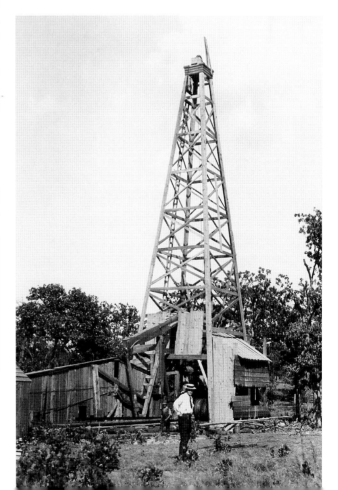

✦ Above: St. Patrick's Mission in Anadarko, as rebuilt after a fire in 1910.
✦ Right: An early Oklahoma oil well.

Ethnic Groups

✧ Holy Family School at Langston, around 1900. At far right is Father Joseph Anciaux, pastor.

AFRICAN AMERICANS

Some 19th century members of the Five Civilized Tribes, including Chickasaws and Seminoles, were slaveholders. After the Civil War black slaves were often adopted into the tribes as freedmen. The opening of the Oklahoma Territory was seen as a heaven-sent opportunity for African Americans, who hoped to create separate towns for black citizens. One entrepreneur in particular, Edwin J. McCabe, founded the city of Langston as a black haven. Though not a Catholic, he approached St. Katharine Drexel in 1891 with a request that she fund a school in Langston. (The public school system did not yet exist then.) She complied, and this was the origin of Holy Family school (and parish) in Langston.

Other missions were founded in Guthrie, Pleasant Valley (in Logan County), Hennessey, Enid, and Oklahoma City, as well as cities in eastern Oklahoma. The civil rights movement had the unfortunate effect of closing those parishes in the name of integration, with a considerable loss of Catholic membership.

HISPANICS

Although many think that the surge in Mexican immigration in Oklahoma is a recent development, Mexican coal miners and smelter workers have labored here since as early as 1914. Carmelite priests, exiled by the Mexican Revolution, also came in 1914; and they established Spanish-speaking missions in Oklahoma City beginning in 1921. At present there are numerous parishes throughout the archdiocese that provide services for Hispanic farm workers and urban laborers.

✧ A few of the Carmelite Fathers, around 1950.

IRISH

The first Irishmen to enter the Oklahoma Territory came as builders of railroads. Most of them had already been in the U.S. for twenty years or more. The oil industry attracted a great many Irish, in every sector of that economy, from oil field workers to tycoons. Many of Oklahoma's most distinguished Catholics, including three of its first four bishops, have been of Irish descent.

GERMANS

The succession of Land Runs in Oklahoma drew many immigrants from Europe. In 1889 alone, some 10,000 came through the port of Liverpool, England. Earlier German migrations had been colonization ventures, where an entrepreneur would buy up a vast tract of land in Texas or Kansas, then sell quarter-section farms acreages to prospective groups emigrating en masse. But this did not happen in Oklahoma. ●●●

✧ Cornerstone laying at Okarche's Holy Trinity, 1902.

●●● Most German farmers who came here had already settled in such places as Iowa or Ohio before they staked their claims in the Sooner State. Once the proper techniques were understood for cultivating the Great Plains, wheat farming became a major occupation for German Catholics. A chain of towns along the 98th Meridian —U.S. Highway 81— is notable for its solid Catholic parishes comprised of farm families, many of them of German descent.

POLES

Following the 1891 Land Run, a colony of Polish farmers from Arkansas settled in what would become the eastern part of Oklahoma County. This was the origin of St. Teresa's parish in Harrah. It is still a strong center of Polish Catholicism.

CZECHS

✧ Bishop McGuinness dedicates a memorial at the National Shrine of the Infant of Prague.

At the time of the Land Runs, the Czech Republic was the Kingdom of Bohemia. Although Bohemia's religious history was turbulent and resulted in a kind of pre-Reformation Protestantism, many Bohemians remained loyal to the Faith. The parishes at Prague, Mishak, Yukon, and Bison owe their development to Bohemian settlers in Oklahoma at the end of the 19th century.

PEOPLE

Black & Indian Missions

✧ The original buildings of St. Patrick's, Anadarko.

On the same day that Bishop Meerschaert was ordained a bishop in Mississippi, a young monk set out from Sacred Heart to establish a mission on the Wichita and Caddo reservation. Several denominations attempted to found schools in the vicinity of Anadarko, but St. Patrick's was the only one that succeeded, due in no small measure to the energy and determination of its founder, Father Isidore Ricklin, O.S.B., and to the financial assistance of Mother Katharine Drexel. St. Patrick's was also the last Catholic Indian mission in Oklahoma to close its doors, lasting until 1966.

Other Catholic mission schools in central and western Oklahoma included St. Elizabeth's School for Chickasaw Girls, Purcell (1888-1948), St. Joseph's Academy, Chickasha (1899-1968), St. Joseph's Academy, Guthrie (1892-1955), St. Agnes Academy, Ardmore (1899-1955), Holy Family, Langston (1895-1924), Sacred Heart (1877-1954), St. Benedict Industrial School for Boys (1880-1901), St. Mary's Academy for Girls (1880-1946), St. Catherine, Guthrie (1896-1918, 1947-1966), Claver College, Guthrie (1933-1944).

The Catholic Church also operated Indian mission schools at the following locations in eastern Oklahoma: Antlers, Hominy Creek (Gray Horse), Muskogee, Quapaw, Pawhuska, Tulsa, and Vinita. All of these were funded in whole or in part by St. Katharine Drexel.

Bishop Meerschaert

THEOPHILE MEERSCHAERT was born in the village of Russignies, East Flanders, Belgium, on August 24, 1847, the second youngest of nine children of a French-speaking Flemish family. (His name is pronounced, more or less, as TAY-oh-feel MEER-shkaart, but in America he used an easier pronunciation: MEER-shirt.) When he was twelve he began seminary studies for the diocesan priesthood, then switched to the American College at the University of Louvain, which trained men to serve as missionaries in the jungles of darkest America. He had his choice of U.S. dioceses, and he chose Natchez, being ordained in Belgium on December 23, 1871. Once in Mississippi he worked in the state's Creole Gulf area, making his way through swamps and nursing yellow fever victims. Eventually he became vicar general of Natchez and rector of its cathedral. It was there he was consecrated a bishop, having been appointed, in April 1891, apostolic vicar of the Indian Territory.

He arrived in Guthrie, the territorial capital and his designated seat, to an enthusiastic reception that featured the governor, the mayor, and a brass band. Then he settled down to 32 years of riding buggies and trains to Stonewall, Antlers, Hinton, Enid, and all points between. He also made a lifetime total of 23 Atlantic crossings on his way to and from Europe where he raised money, recruited priests and seminarians, and reported to his superiors in Rome. He kept a detailed diary that tells us much about the growth of Oklahoma and Catholicism from territory days to statehood and beyond. He died in Oklahoma City, at the age of 76, on February 24, 1924.

St. Katharine Drexel

THE Drexel banking fortune began in 1837, founded in Philadelphia by Francis Martin Drexel. His son, Anthony Joseph Drexel, outlived two wives before himself dying at age 42. At his death in 1885, he left three unmarried daughters, who jointly inherited his estate of $15,000.000. The second of these was Catherine Mary, born November 28, 1858, and 26 years old at the time of her father's death. One of her sisters soon after died in childbirth, and the other married a Philadelphia banker. This left Catherine in effect in control of the entire estate.

The Drexels were exemplary Catholics. Catherine and her sisters considered the needs of minority peoples, even visiting Western reservations and city ghettos. In 1887 they founded their first two missions, one of them for Osage girls at Pawhuska and the second at Purcell for Chickasaw children. In 1890 Catherine entered a convent in Pittsburgh and the next year she became the first professed sister in her own order, the Sisters of the Blessed Sacrament for Indians and Colored People. Between 1902 and 1931 Mother Mary Katharine Drexel —she changed the spelling when she took her vows— visited Oklahoma several times, checking on her mission schools, including those at Purcell, Anadarko, Ardmore, Langston, Chickasha, and Guthrie. Over the years she spent millions of dollars on some 60 schools throughout the South and the West, of which the best known is Xavier University in New Orleans. She died on March 3, 1955, at the age of 96. Because of her generous and holy life, the cause of her canonization was quickly taken up. She was beatified in 1988 and canonized on October 1, 2000. Her feast day is March 3.

4 Diocese of Oklahoma

August 17, 1905 - November 14, 1930

THE Church's usual practice, when it creates an apostolic vicariate, is to move fairly quickly toward conferring full diocesan status on the missionary region already entrusted to a bishop. In the case of Oklahoma, however, the vicariate period lasted all of fourteen years, in spite of the best efforts of Bishop Meerschaert, the archbishop of New Orleans, and the other bishops of the New Orleans province to move things forward.

The delay was caused by infighting between Meerschaert and the Benedictines of Sacred Heart, especially their abbot, Dom Felix DeGrasse. The monks had never fully accepted the transfer of their prefecture to a diocesan bishop, and there were a few outstanding questions of jurisdiction, especially regarding parishes in the McAlester area. Abbot DeGrasse chose to make an issue of these, and he had powerful friends among Benedictine superiors in Rome. He died in January 1905, however, and the abbot who came from Europe to preside at the election of his successor was open to discussing the issue with Meerschaert. When the bishop went to Rome that summer to report on the state of things in Oklahoma, he came away assured that the obstacles were removed.

So it was that in 1905, two years before statehood, the local Church was given full status as the Diocese of Oklahoma, and Oklahoma City was named its

❖ Bishop Meerschaert's private chapel.

diocesan seat. Meerschaert continued to lead the new jurisdiction until his death in 1924.

During his time in Oklahoma, an issue of national importance arose in what came to be known as the Sacramental Wine Case. This stemmed from the state legislature's decision to ban the manufacture or import of alcoholic beverages. No religious exemption was made, nor was one applied for. Not until priests found themselves actually unable to obtain altar wine for Mass, in fact, did the diocese appeal for relief from the courts. The state Supreme Court decided in the Church's favor in May 1918, in a case that was closely watched on both sides of the then-developing national debate over Prohibition.

❖ In 1905 Bishop Meerschaert sat for this portrait with the Benedictine community at Sacred Heart. The occasion was the blessing of Abbot Bernard Murphy (at the bishop's left).

They Made a Difference

MSGR. WILLIAM H. KETCHAM

Born in Iowa (1869-1921), he migrated to Texas with his parents as a small boy. He joined the Church in high school, then entered the seminary. In 1889 his family moved again, this time to the Indian Territory. When Bishop Meerschaert arrived in Guthrie, Ketcham, by now nearly finished with his studies, applied for permission to be a priest in the new vicariate. He thus became the first priest Meerschaert ordained, in March 1892. After pastorates in Muskogee and Antlers, he was selected in 1900 as assistant to the director of the Catholic Bureau of Indian Missions, in Washington, D.C. The director retired the next year, and Ketcham succeeded him, serving for twenty years in the post. As director he was closely associated with St. Katharine Drexel, the chief benefactor of the Bureau. Theodore Roosevelt and William Howard Taft were impressed with him, and Taft named him to the U.S. Board of Indian Commissioners. His sudden death at 53 robbed the Church, and Native Americans generally, of a competent and devoted servant.

MSGR. GUSTAVE DEPREITERE

Gustave Depreitere (1871-1961) hailed from Courtrai, Belgium; his mother was Bishop Meerschaert's sister. He was ordained in 1895. Ten years later the bishop appointed him vicar general—second in command—of the newly constituted Diocese of Oklahoma; he held this post for a remarkable fifty-six years, administering the diocese after his uncle's death in 1924. He established the parish in Enid, and he was pastor of St. Joseph's Old Cathedral for forty years. His own nephew, Father Emil Depreitere, was ordained in Oklahoma in 1918.

REVEREND STANLEY FRANCIS ROTHER

Born in Okarche, Stanley Rother (1935-1981) had a hard time in the seminary. Only Bishop Reed's faith in him brought him through to ordination. In 1968 he joined the Oklahoma priests at work at the diocesan mission in Santiago Atitlan, Guatemala. Within a few years he was the only priest remaining at the mission, and he determined to give the remainder of his life to the people of Santiago Atitlan. He did so on July 28, 1981, when he was murdered in his rectory by one of the death squads that were then terrorizing the Guatemalan people. His name has since been submitted to the Holy See for consideration as a possible saint.

MSGR. DON J. KANALY

He was the grandson (1905-1995) of a pioneer who made the 1893 Land Run into Oklahoma. He attended seminary at the American College of the University of Louvain, Belgium, where he became acquainted with the thought of Canon (later cardinal) Joseph Cardijn, and its implications for reinvigorating the Christian spirit of the laity. Ordained in 1938, he returned home and, with the full support of Bishop Kelley, started the first American chapters of the Young Christian Workers, the Young Christian Students, and the Christian Family Movement. In the 1940's he directed a catechetical correspondence school for children living outside Oklahoma's cities. As pastor of St. Patrick's in Oklahoma City, he led his people in realizing the dream of a landmark church built by the parishioners themselves.

MSGR. ZENON STEBER

A native of Alsace (1870-1948), a border province over which France and Germany fought three wars, Zenon Steber—ZAY-nohn stay-BEAR is the accepted pronunciation among

Oklahomans—was ordained a priest for the African missions in 1893. His health failed him on the Gold Coast, however, and he came to Oklahoma, looking for the most demanding kind of missionary work. He found it in southwestern Oklahoma, where his parish encompassed six counties and 24,000 square miles. From 1902 to 1948 he was pastor of Okarche, where he built Holy Trinity Church and one of the most solidly Catholic towns in all of Oklahoma.

REVEREND CHARLES H. SCHETTLER

Born on a farm near Sterling in 1929, Father Schettler was ordained in Rome in 1954. Throughout practically all of the intervening half century, he has labored in the archdiocesan marriage tribunal, where he has brought his knowledge of Church law to the pastoral task of helping Catholics with legally problematic marriages to resume the full sacramental life of the Church. Literally thousands of Catholic spouses owe their lives of grace to his unsung work on their behalf.

REVEREND DAVID F. MONAHAN

After two decades as a pastor and educator—he was diocesan superintendent of schools from 1970 to 1974—Father Monahan (born 1927, ordained 1952) began a new career as the first editor of The Sooner Catholic, which he quickly developed into one of the nation's finest biweekly publications. A newspaperman at once trenchant and gentle, he stimulated the thinking of Oklahoma's Catholics about the issues of the day, and his remarkable gift for lively story telling spread before us the table of our common heritage.

REVEREND GREGORY GERRER, O.S.B.

Robert Gerrer (1867-1946) was born, like Msgr. Steber, in Alsace, but he emigrated with his family to the U.S. at the age of four. He pursued several careers, even playing the clarinet in a circus band, before deciding on the monastery, where he was

given the name Gregory. While he was still in formation, Sacred Heart Abbey burned down and the monks were dispersed. A talented artist, Father Gregory was sent to Rome to further his studies. While there, he won the chance to paint the official portrait of the newly elected Pope, St. Pius X. His original painting is now in the museum in Shawnee that bears his name, while a copy hangs in the Vatican. His contacts with other young artists of that time and place resulted in St. Gregory's Abbey becoming the possessor of a superlative collection of Impressionist oils. In 1918 he became the founder and curator of the Wightman Memorial Art Gallery at Notre Dame University.

REVEREND JOHN A. PETUSKEY

An extrovert par excellence, Father Petuskey (1938-2003) was born in New Jersey and ordained in Oklahoma City in 1966. As diocesan superintendent of schools, he was an avid proponent of parish-based education. He fought the Oklahoma education establishment and obtained Catholic students' proper share of federal funds for supplemental programs. It is as an unforgettable pastor in Guthrie, Oklahoma City, and Edmond, however, that he will remain in the hearts of Catholic Oklahomans.

REVEREND RAMON CARLIN

When he was born in Haskell (1916-1977), his parents named him Raymond, but he always had an affinity for Spanish and for Hispanics, and he called himself Ramon for so long that people thought it really was his name. Ordained in 1941, he was a pastor in the missions of eastern Oklahoma, a chaplain in a federal reformatory and an instructor in the diocesan high school. In 1963 he undertook his greatest work, that of leading a band of Oklahomans to establish the diocesan mission at Santiago Atitlan, Guatemala. This involved learning the native dialect, Tzutuhil, which he then systematized so that other missionaries could learn to read and write it, too. Eventually he began a language school in Guatemala. Along the way, he made improvements in the villagers' health care, education, and liturgical participation.

5 Oklahoma City & Tulsa
November 14, 1930 - February 6, 1973

EERSCHAERT'S successor, Bishop Francis Clement Kelley (1924-1948) was, in his day, probably Oklahoma's best-known churchman. With twenty years of experience in fundraising and publishing behind him by the time he came to Oklahoma, he was a force to be reckoned with. His first five years were indeed productive, as he reorganized and revitalized a diocese that had grown content with small victories.

He was especially impressed with Tulsa, which was then approaching its zenith as the Oil Capital of the World. At one point he considered moving his residence and chancery there, but when he saw this was impracticable, he determined that Tulsa should at least have its own cathedral and equal billing with Oklahoma City in the diocesan title. He petitioned the Holy See that the Diocese of Oklahoma should be restyled the Diocese of Oklahoma City and Tulsa. This took effect at the end of 1930.

Kelley had every reason to suppose that his early years in office would be the prelude to his advancement. As founder and head of Catholic Extension, however, he had not only saved the Church

⊕ For years the 250-foot main steeple of Holy Family Cathedral was one of Tulsa's tallest structures.

A MAJOR concern of the bishops of Oklahoma has been to supply men and women to serve the needs of the far-flung parishes and special ministries throughout the central and western areas of the state. An archdiocesan vocations office provides opportunities for young people to discern their own life's work, and recruiting priests, whether from Oklahoma or out-of-state, is an ongoing process.

A provision of the Second Vatican Council's Constitution on the Church (Lumen Gentium, para. 29) allowed for the restoration of the Order of Deacons as a permanent state in life, not merely as the last step before priesthood. It specifically allowed for candidates who were married.

Pope Paul VI issued an implementing decree in 1972, and throughout the United States dioceses began the process of explaining the diaconate concept to priests and laity, setting up training programs, recruiting men for the first classes, and helping them prepare spiritually and skillfully for the varied works they would be doing.

Archbishop Salatka ordained the first group of seven candidates in Oklahoma City on June 24, 1978. Since then the deacons, who form a separate and complementary order to the Order of Presbyters (priests), have become a valued resource for the archbishops, priests, and people of the archdiocese. In 2004, in the archdiocese of Oklahoma City, there were 71 permanent deacons working with 134 diocesan and religious priests and 124 religious sisters.

---

in rural America, he had also made enemies among highly-placed clerics. The result was that a promotion he had assumed was his, to the archbishopric of Dubuque, instead went to someone else. In 1930, just as the Depression struck Oklahoma, drying up farms and sending oil prices plunging, Kelley came to see that he was destined to live out his days in a small and impoverished midwestern diocese.

His goal became the simple one of remaining financially solvent. He was a prolific author and speaker, and throughout the 1930's he gave numerous retreats and published one book after another to produce income for his diocese. He was gone so much that his priests called him "the bishop *from* Oklahoma." In a profoundly ironic development, this hero of the American home missions found himself faced with having to close dozens of small mission parishes throughout Oklahoma, because he had neither the funds nor the priests to supply them. He managed, though, to bring the diocese through the Depression in one piece. The archdiocese of Dubuque, on the other hand, went bankrupt.

✧ Top right: The first permanent deacons of the archdiocese, ordained in June 1978.
✧ Bottom right: Oklahoma's bishops have always been concerned to provide pastors for their parishes. Here Bishop Reed meets with a group of vocation-minded laymen.

Bishop Kelley's undeniable talent proved inadequate to realize his main program in Oklahoma, which was to increase Catholic population through evangelization. At his death in 1948, Oklahoma Catholics were estimated to be approximately 73,000, out of a total population of 2,500,000, or about three per cent. This modest increase from 1891 appears to be based largely on the birthrate. The predominating culture of the state, expressed in its populist philosophy and religious fundamentalism, had proven resistant to Catholic missionary inroads.

Kelley was followed in office by Bishop Eugene J. McGuinness, who had served as Kelley's vice-president at the Extension Society. Consecrated

bishop of Raleigh, North Carolina, in 1937, he came to Oklahoma in 1945 as apostolic administrator following Kelley's decline in health. Recognizing that there was no hope of evangelizing the state without a significant increase of Oklahoma-born vocations, he made recruitment to the priesthood and religious life the chief focus of his episcopate. Helped in part by the optimistic atmosphere of the postwar years, and by his own infectious enthusiasm, he achieved considerable success in this effort. In 1945 the diocese had but five seminarians. At McGuinness' death in December 1957 there were twenty-six, and ordination classes of ten or twelve a year were becoming commonplace. Given the comparatively large number of adult converts during this same period, it may be said that the 1950's marked an institutional high point of Oklahoma's diocesan development.

Oklahoma's fourth bishop was the urbane and affable Victor J. Reed (1958-1971), born in Indiana but an Oklahoman from the age of five. He inherited a diocesan church that was buoyed by its recent achievements and looking forward to further successes. These rising expectations, unrealistic to a degree and inflated further by the promised reforms of the Second Vatican Council, were severely depressed by the assassination of John Kennedy and the nation's involvement in Vietnam. By the middle 1960's men and women were defecting from Catholic ministry in Oklahoma at a rate seemingly higher than in the country as a whole. (This phenomenon, however, came nearly to a stop in Oklahoma several years before it did in the rest of the nation.) Bishop Reed trusted and encouraged his priests and laity. Perhaps inevitably, he was hurt by the failure of many of them to meet his own expectations. He demonstrated his moral leadership on several occasions, most notably in 1967, when he became the first American Catholic bishop publicly to protest the Vietnam War.

Reed's episcopate was strongly influenced by a financial calamity. The Benedictine Sisters in Tulsa had built a new college, but found themselves unable to pay for it. The diocese had to step in and take over the payments. (This brought about, in 1962, the genesis of the Archdiocesan Development Fund.) The mortgage was finally paid off in 1971, and the bishop turned his attention to another matter of importance—dividing the diocese. He was laying the foundation for this move when he suffered a fatal stroke on September 7, 1971.

Catholic Extension

Bishop Kelley

more than 10,000 Catholic churches throughout the rural United States by the end of the century.

When he was appointed Bishop of Oklahoma in 1924, he was already a highly influential churchman. He attended the Versailles Peace Conference in 1919 on behalf of the missions of German Southwest Africa (modern Namibia) and, through conversations in Paris with the foreign minister of Italy, was instrumental in breaking the impasse between the Holy See and the government of Italy over the Roman Question, leading to the creation in 1929 of the Vatican City State. He was a prolific author (17 books, dozens of articles in Extension magazine and elsewhere), and a superb orator.

He had made enemies, too, and his appointment to a small midwestern diocese was not so much a promotion as an attempt to remove him from the national stage. His first years in office were promising, but the Depression and his long final illness made significant progress meager.

He was more successful in his efforts on behalf of the Church outside his state. The Mexican Revolution in 1910 set that nation on a long road of social development whose mirror image was official hatred of the Church, its priests, and its property. Many Mexican priests and bishops had to flee for their lives, and Francis Kelley became the American spokesman for their plight. While still at Extension he had underwritten the establishment in Texas of a Mexican seminary-in-exile, and as treasurer of the American bishops' national conference he was active in creating a permanent successor institution, the Montezuma Seminary in New Mexico.

F RANCIS Clement Kelley's birth date is a matter of some guesswork, because record-keeping in 19ᵗʰ-century Canada was still rather primitive. As best we —or Kelley himself— could determine, he entered the world at Vernon River, in the Maritime province of Prince Edward Island, probably on October 23, 1870. Like Bishop Meerschaert, he was ordained for a U.S. diocese—in his case, Detroit—on August 24, 1893. Five years later he signed up as a chaplain during the Spanish-American War, and he earned extra money for his Michigan parish by lecturing about his experiences.

His lecture tour brought him to places like Ellsworth, Kansas, where a tumbledown church and a desperate priest made him realize the need for a national organization that would provide funds to keep the Church alive there. In 1905 he founded the Catholic Church Extension Society under the patronage of the archbishop of Chicago, where he established an office, a magazine, and a highly successful fundraising effort that, among other things, would build

One of the ironies of his life was that changing economic and population patterns meant that this apostle of the rural Church was forced to close dozens of small country parishes throughout Oklahoma. By the time of his death, on February 1, 1948, he had given retreats and lectures all over the country, thus managing to keep his diocese from going bankrupt during the years after 1930.

Bishop McGuinness

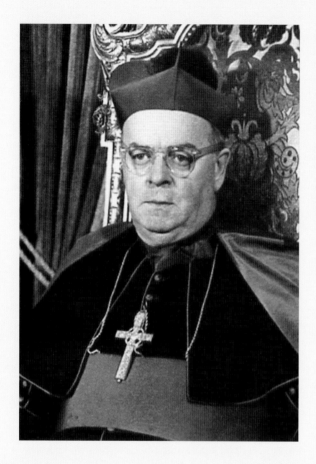

✧ Fred Lookout, principal chief of the Osages, was over 80 when Bishop McGuinness baptized him in Pawhuska in 1945.

home in the Philadelphia area. (A curious sidelight of this was that many congregations were surprised, on the day their new churches were dedicated, to find that the church, and consequently the parish, had received a new name, the result of donors' wishes being honored.)

A major event during his episcopate was the golden jubilee of the diocese, celebrated in October 1955. A church that had kept its head down under the pressure of anti-Catholic bias suddenly projected itself onto the consciousness of Oklahomans statewide. A large outdoor Mass at the Oklahoma City fairgrounds was preceded by a parade through the downtown by several thousand elementary and high school students singing that they were "an army of youth, flying the standards of truth ... [and] fighting for Christ the Lord."

The following year the diocese saw its most intensive effort ever at evangelizing Oklahomans. Operation Understanding saw an open house in every parish, with parishioners giving guided tours of their churches and answering questions from interested non-Catholics.

O KLAHOMA's third bishop was born Eugene Joseph McGuinness in Hellerton, Pennsylvania, on September 6, 1889. Ordained for the archdiocese of Philadelphia on May 22, 1915, his interest in the missions led him to work for Francis Kelley and the Extension Society, where he became vice-president of Catholic Extension. In 1937 he was named bishop of Raleigh, North Carolina, and seven years later he was asked to come to Oklahoma as assistant to the ailing Bishop Kelley. From the moment he arrived in January 1945 he became responsible for the government of the diocese, bishop in all but name until Kelley's death three years later.

His thirteen years in Oklahoma coincided with a period of national expansion after World War II, and he was able to pursue his goals of establishing new parishes and ordaining priests to serve in them. He hated debt, and so he paid off many mission churches with the help of donors from Extension and from his

An effervescent man, Bishop Mc Guiness was tireless in his promotion of vocations, which led eventually to his life's dream, a seminary in Oklahoma City. He lived long enough to see it started, but he died suddenly on December 27, 1957, at the age of 68.

Bishop Reed

VICTOR Joseph Reed was one of Oklahoma's own. Though born in Montpelier, Indiana (on December 23, 1905), he came to Oklahoma at the age of five with his family because of his father's connection to the oil business. The Reeds settled in Tulsa, and young Victor attended elementary and high school at St. Joseph's College in Muskogee. Ordained in Rome on December 21, 1929, Father Reed became involved in many of the social causes that preoccupied the Church in Oklahoma and the world in the 1920's and 1930's. With fellow curate Father Stephen Leven, he pioneered in Catholic street-preaching in Oklahoma City and throughout the state. In the years 1935-39 he was in Europe again for studies at the University of Louvain, where he earned a doctorate in philosophy.

He served as pastor in Stillwater and Tulsa before his episcopal appointment as auxiliary to Bishop McGuinness in December 1957. McGuinness' death three weeks later meant that Reed was chosen to administer the diocese in the interval between bishops; this in turn led to his appointment as fourth bishop of Oklahoma in January 1958. His ordination occurred at Holy Family Co-Cathedral in Tulsa on March 5, and he was installed at Our Lady of Perpetual Help Cathedral, Oklahoma City, on March 19, the feast of St. Joseph, patron of the diocese.

His tenure as bishop was shaped, first of all, by the Second Vatican Council—whose four sessions in Rome, 1962 through 1965, he attended—and then by the period of high popular expectations mixed with disappointment that followed. Another major factor in his episcopate was economic, because the diocese was forced to take over a large indebtedness to forestall bankruptcy of the Benedictine Sisters in Tulsa following their construction of a junior college. (This provided the impetus for the Archdiocesan Development Fund.)

As priests and sisters became exasperated at the slow pace of reform, laypeople were horrified by changes in a Church they had grown to believe was unchangeable. Basically a political conservative, Bishop Reed was faced with the need to respond to the challenges of the civil rights movement and the Vietnam War. He became the first American bishop to question the war publicly when in 1967 he signed a petition urging negotiation to bring it to an end.

For this and other controversial stances, the bishop found himself severely criticized from within and outside of the Church. Although he found the almost ceaseless attacks hurtful, he remained serenely steadfast in his leadership of the Oklahoma Church. His death came early and suddenly, the result of a stroke, on September 8, 1971.

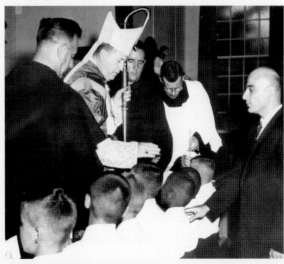

◈ Bishop Victor Reed, assisted by two Holy Ghost Fathers, confirms a group of African American boys.

Hospitals

Possibly the greatest impact of the Catholic Church upon the ordinary citizen of Oklahoma has been through its system of Catholic hospitals. The first hospital in the Oklahoma Territory was founded under Catholic auspices. Some hospitals were begun at the insistence of pastors who were concerned that no facilities existed in their areas for the care of the sick. Beginning around 1935, and for some thirty years thereafter, a number of medium-sized cities in Oklahoma, finding themselves unable to support local hospitals with civic resources, offered them to Catholic religious orders to operate. The current movement toward Health Management Organizations (HMO's) has led Catholic hospitals to join in providing more efficient services to large numbers of Oklahomans.

ST. ANTHONY HOSPITAL, OKLAHOMA CITY

Currently a 684-bed, non-profit general hospital, St. Anthony owes its beginning to Father Ildephonse Lanslots, O.S.B., pastor of St. Joseph Church in Oklahoma City. Recognizing the need for medical facilities in the rapidly growing city, he asked the Sisters of St. Francis of Maryville, Missouri, to establish a hospital. The 600 block of West Ninth Street was purchased on July 14, 1898, and a 12-bed hospital opened in temporary quarters on Fourth Street on August 1. Since these rooms were unheated, the sisters decided to close the hospital in November, only to open it in a new brick building a year later. The hospital has been operating ever since, the oldest hospital in continuing operation in Oklahoma.

In 1908, St. Anthony's opened a diploma training school in nursing. In 1925 it instituted the first hospital pharmacy in the state. Major renovations were carried out in 1906, 1909, 1972, and 1979. St. Anthony's is a member of the SSM Health Care System and sponsored by the Franciscan Sisters of Mary, St. Louis, Missouri.

BLACKWELL REGIONAL HOSPITAL, BLACKWELL

A girls' dormitory at a Baptist college was built in 1909; at a sheriff's sale in 1912 the building was purchased by three doctors and operated as Blackwell Hospital from 1914 to 1940. It was then purchased by the city. In 1946, the Felician Sisters of Lodi, New Jersey, accepted ownership and management until a new hospital was built in 1955. The new structure, Blackwell Regional Hospital, was run by the Felician Sisters until 1975, when they sold it to the Sisters of St. Joseph of Wichita, who merged it with St. Joseph's Regional Medical Center of Northern Oklahoma, located in Ponca City, until 1986. That year the City of Blackwell arranged to secure the facility and lease it to the Baptist Health Care Corporation of Oklahoma.

ST. JOSEPH REGIONAL MEDICAL CENTER OF NORTHEAST OKLAHOMA, INC., PONCA CITY

In 1919 the Ponca City Chamber of Commerce established the 14-bed Ponca City Hospital in a frame building at 403 West Grand Avenue. In January 1921 the hospital was given to the Sisters of St. Joseph of Wichita, free of debt, and they assumed management. A fund drive led by the Chamber of Commerce, E.W. Marland, and the Marland Oil Company provided $250,000 toward the construction of a new hospital which began in 1925 at the present site, 14th and Hartford.

In 1975 the Ponca City Hospital changed its name to St. Joseph Regional Medical Center of Ponca City, Inc. In July 1983 the hospital assumed its current name, St. Joseph Regional Medical Center of Northeast Oklahoma, Inc. A 203-bed non-profit general hospital, it is owned and operated by the Sisters of St. Joseph of Wichita through the CSJ Health System of Wichita, Kansas.

ST. MARY'S MERCY HOSPITAL, ENID

On June 1, 1937, the Enid Springs Sanitarium and Bathhouse was purchased from a group of physicians by the Sisters Adorers of the Most Precious Blood. In 1940 the original hospital was removed after a new addition was completed, and the following year the name was changed to St. Mary's Hospital of Enid, Oklahoma. Major expansion and renovation projects were completed in 1949, 1953, 1963, 1966, 1968, 1972, 1975, and 1982. In 1984 the 277-bed general hospital was leased and operated by Hospital Corporation of America, Nashville, Tennessee. It was bought by the Sisters of Mercy Health System but later sold and is no longer a Catholic hospital.

VILLA MADONNA, ENID

University Hospital, at first privately owned and then a Baptist institution, was sold to the Sisters Adorers of the Most Precious Blood in 1946. A 32-bed convalescent hospital, it was known as St. Mary's Hospital Annex, then as Villa Madonna. It closed in 1969.

BENEDICTINE HEIGHTS HOSPITAL (ALVERNO HEIGHTS HOSPITAL), GUTHRIE

A 55-bed, non-profit general hospital was begun in 1947 by the Cimarron Valley Wesley Hospital; the unfinished framework was purchased in 1948 by the Benedictine Sisters, with a grant from the Katherine E. Price Foundation of New York. The Benedictines operated it until 1964. That year they sold it to the Sisters of St. Francis of Maryville, Missouri, who renamed it Alverno Heights Hospital and operated it as an adjunct of St. Anthony's Hospital, Oklahoma City, until 1972, when it was sold to the Logan County Memorial Hospital.

OKARCHE MEMORIAL HOSPITAL, OKARCHE

A 25-bed municipally owned general hospital was built in Okarche in 1946. In 1949 the facility was leased to the Felician Sisters who operated it until 1986. They completed a major renovation in 1965. The hospital was leased to the Baptist Health Care Corporation of Oklahoma in 1986.

MERCY HEALTH CENTER, OKLAHOMA CITY

The Sisters of Mercy of the Union purchased the old Oklahoma City General Hospital (formerly the Baptist Hospital) at 501 N.W. Twelfth Street in 1947. They renamed the 147-bed facility

Mercy Hospital. In 1974, under the direction of Sister Mary Coletta Massoth, R.S.M., the sisters constructed a 432-bed general hospital, Mercy Health Center, at 4300 West Memorial Road. The original cost was $28 million, but major expansion and renovation was carried out in 1982 and 1985.

BONE AND JOINT HOSPITAL, OKLAHOMA CITY

Originally known as McBride's Reconstruction Hospital and located at Seventh and North Robinson since 1926, the name was changed to the Bone and Joint Hospital when it was moved to a new facility at 605 N.W. Tenth Street in 1938. This facility in turn was leveled in 1979 to make room for a new hospital with 102 beds. In 1976 its assets were acquired by the Oklahoma Orthopedic and Arthritis Foundation, but at present it is a member of the Sisters of Mercy Health Care System and sponsored by the Franciscan Sisters of Mary, St. Louis, Missouri.

MERCY MEMORIAL HEALTH CENTER, ARDMORE

In 1898, the first hospital established between Oklahoma City and Fort Worth, Texas, opened in Ardmore. Since then the city has hosted more than a dozen hospitals, including successor institutions. In 1955 the Memorial Hospital of Southern Oklahoma with 100 beds was built. The cost was $1.3 million which was financed by local contributions and a federal Hill-Burton grant. The hospital subsequently expanded to 163 beds through projects completed in 1960, 1972, 1980, 1984 and 1986.

In 1996, management and ownership of the hospital was transferred to the Sisters of Mercy Health System, Saint Louis, Missouri. Under this subsidiary of the Sisters of Mercy, a new ambulatory surgery center opened in 2002.

ST. MICHAEL HOSPITAL, OKLAHOMA CITY

Located at 2129 S.W. 59th Street in Oklahoma City, this hospital was originally built in 1955 as the Hillcrest Osteopathic Hospital, a privately owned facility. In 1986 the 148-bed general hospital became Hillcrest Medical Center. It is now a member of the SSM Health Care System and sponsored by the Franciscan Sisters of Mary, St. Louis, Missouri.

Bishop McGuinness High School

*I*N the late 1940's Catholic parishes were multiplying in Oklahoma City. Teenagers in such parishes lived too far from establshed Catholic high schools sponsored by older parishes. This led to the decision to close the parish-based high schools and open a single, central school that would bring Catholic students together in an environment more supportive of their faith.

To this end property was purchased at 50th and Western, and in September 1950 the new school opened with 300 students. At first the facility was given the cheery name of Catholic Hi, but following the death of the bishop who had brought the project along, its name was changed to Bishop McGuinness High School.

After years of expansions and renovations, the crowning edifice of the school, the Frassati Chapel, was dedicated in 1998. The chapel was named for Blessed Pier Giorgio Frassati

(1901-1924); an Italian athlete and youth advocate who died of polio as a result of working with the poor. He was the choice of a student/faculty vote conducted to choose a patron saint for the chapel.

In 2004, an extensive capital campaign was inaugurated to replace many of the aging and deteriorating campus facilities.

Mount Saint Mary High School

*O*N the night of January 15, 1901, around 11:00, a fire broke out in the dining room of the monastery and school complex at Sacred Heart Abbey. Within a few hours the whole campus, built entirely of frame construction, lay in ruins. Among the buildings destroyed was St. Mary's Academy and the convent of the Sisters of Mercy.

By the turn of the 20th century it was evident that Oklahoma City would be the center of the emerging new state, and that if St. Mary's was to be rebuilt it should rise there. In 1903 the sisters, aided by a grant of land on Capitol Hill, the highest point in the city, began construction of a remarkable Victorian structure that even today merits its title, "the Castle on the Hill." Mount Saint Mary's is now the oldest high school in Oklahoma.

When Bishop McGuinness decreed the consolidation of Catholic high schools in favor of a single, centrally-located facility, he exempted Mount Saint Mary's because it was

situated south of the North Canadian River, quite far from the intended location of the new school. As Mount Saint Mary's celebrated its centennial, a campaign has begun to update the venerable institution and ready it for its second hundred years of service to Oklahoma City.

6 *Archdiocese & Province*

February 6, 1973 - Present

A T 42, Bishop John R. Quinn was the American Church's youngest ordinary (ruling bishop) when, in January 1972, he took office in Oklahoma City as its fifth bishop. He quickly showed himself to be a meticulous theologian and prudent administrator, deftly handling challenges from both ends of the spectrum of ecclesiastical and civil politics. It was no surprise that after only five years in Oklahoma, he was named archbishop of San Francisco. He was installed there in April 1977. A few months later he was elected president of the National Conference of Catholic Bishops.

On December 19, 1972, it was announced that the long-awaited division of the Oklahoma diocese had taken place, and moreover, that a new ecclesiastical province had been created. Bishop Quinn was named the first Archbishop of Oklahoma City, in which post he was installed on February 6, 1973. The diocese of Little Rock and the new diocese of Tulsa were designated as suffragan sees of the new province.

The founding bishop of Tulsa was Monsignor Bernard J. Ganter, a priest of the diocese of Galveston-Houston and, at the time of his appointment, chancellor of that see. He was ordained bishop in Holy Family Cathedral on February 7, 1973. On the same day the new diocese, comprising some 51,000 Catholics in 31 of Oklahoma's 77 counties, was formally established.

The second archbishop of Oklahoma City was Most Reverend Charles A. Salatka, born in Grand Rapids, Michigan, and ordained a priest of the Grand Rapids diocese in 1945. He had been auxiliary bishop of Grand Rapids (1962-1968) and bishop of Marquette (1968-1977) prior to his appointment in Oklahoma. When his resignation was announced in November

❖ Archbishop Salatka greets Oklahoma City parishioners upon his arrival in 1977.

1992, he was the senior bishop, in years of ordination, in the United States. He died in Oklahoma City on March 17, 2003.

In Tulsa, Bishop Ganter was followed by Monsignor Eusebius J. Beltran, vicar general of the archdiocese of Atlanta, Georgia. Bishop Beltran, a priest since 1960, was ordained bishop in Tulsa on April 20, 1978, by Archbishop Salatka. Bishop Beltran is credited with a significant expansion in the work of Catholic Charities in Tulsa, for maintaining the remnants of the diocesan system of Catholic schools, and for a successful program of vocations recruitment. On January 22, 1993, Bishop Beltran was installed as third Archbishop of Oklahoma City. His successor in Tulsa was Bishop Edward J. Slattery, a veteran, like Bishops Kelley and McGuinness, of the Catholic Church Extension Society. He was ordained by Pope John Paul II in Rome on January 6, 1994.

❖ Bishop Bernard Ganter hosts Mother Teresa of Calcutta in Tulsa in 1976.

✤ Father John Sullivan, pastor of Guthrie from 1947 to 1959, and afterward national director of the Extension Lay Volunteers, was named a bishop in 1972.

✤ Archbishop Salatka ordains Bishop Eusebius Beltran. The scene is Holy Family Cathedral, Tulsa, in 1978.

Three other bishops have roots in the diocese. Bishops Stephen A. Leven (auxiliary of San Antonio, Texas, 1957-69; ordinary of San Angelo, Texas, 1969-79; died 1983) and Charles A. Buswell (ordinary of Pueblo, Colorado, 1959-79) were Oklahoma natives. Bishop John J. Sullivan (ordinary of Grand Island, Nebraska, 1972-77; and of Kansas City, Missouri, 1977-93; died 2001) was ordained an Oklahoma priest in 1944.

Another Oklahoma priest of note is Father William Henry Ketcham, director of the Bureau of Catholic Indian Missions, Washington, D.C., from 1901 to 1921, and a forceful advocate of Native American rights to Catholic education. Monsignor John J. Walde was the first Catholic priest in the United States to use radio as a forum for preaching Catholic doctrine; the weekly feature began in October 1925 and was broadcast uninterruptedly for 45 years. Monsignor Don J. Kanaly organized the first American chapter of the Young Christian Workers in Ponca City, Oklahoma, in 1939; he also was instrumental in developing the program at the national level. Father Stanley F. Rother served thirteen years in the diocesan mission at Santiago Atitlan, Guatemala, culminating

in his murder by forces of the Guatemalan regime on July 28, 1981.

Among the more important religious communities to have labored in Oklahoma are the Benedictines: the monks of St. Gregory's Abbey, Shawnee, and the nuns of St. Joseph's Monastery, first located in Guthrie and now in Tulsa. St. Gregory's University traces its beginning to 1877. The Benedictine nuns formerly ran secondary and collegiate institutions in Guthrie and Tulsa.

The Mexican revolution brought Carmelite priest refugees to Oklahoma in 1914. A diocesan sisterhood, the Carmelite Sisters of St. Therese, developed from their efforts in 1917. Also notable are the Sisters of Mercy, who established themselves in Oklahoma in 1884; their motherhouse is in Oklahoma City. Numerous other communities of religious men and women have ministered in the state.

Catholic involvement in political life has centered around two time periods, the turn of the century and the present. Among important figures of the earlier period are James Bigheart, chief of the Osage tribe; Dennis T. Flynn, first Congressional delegate from

✧ Left to right: Father Stanley Rother, missionary and martyr of Guatemala; Thomas H. Doyle, judge of the Oklahoma Court of Criminal Appeals; Monsignor John Walde, longtime radio priest; Father John Walch, artist and designer.

the Oklahoma Territory; Kate Barnard, a reformer who was elected Oklahoma's first commissioner of charities and corrections; Matthew Kane and Thomas Doyle, both high ranking members of the Oklahoma judiciary (Kane was chief justice of the state supreme court at the time of the Sacramental Wine Case); and Peter Hanratty, an early advocate and organizer of Oklahoma's coal miners.

More recent Catholic political figures include Dewey Bartlett (governor 1967-71, U.S. senator 1972-79), Don Nickles (U.S. senator 1977-2005), James R. Jones (U.S. representative 1972-86, ambassador to Mexico 1992-2001), David Walters (governor 1991-95), and Frank Keating (governor 1995-2003). Keating also served as first chairman (2002-2003) of the national review board established by the American bishops in the wake of the U.S. sex-abuse scandals.

Oklahoma Catholics in the arts have included Pulitzer Prize-winning poet John Berryman, actress Jennifer Jones (who made her screen debut in the title role of The Song of Bernadette), and ballerinas Maria and Marjorie Tallchief and Yvonne Chouteau. Father Gregory Gerrer, O.S.B., painted the official portrait of Pope St. Pius X in 1904. Father John Walch was a liturgical artist and designer whose works date chiefly from the 1950's and 1960's. Also of note are agronomists Joseph Danne and Father H.B. Mandelartz, who developed important new strains of wheat and corn, respectively.

Oklahoma's population was estimated in 2003 to be 4,170,984. Catholics accounted for 169,045 of this number, or approximately four percent. 112,951 Catholics were numbered in the archdiocese of Oklahoma City, and 56,094 in the diocese of Tulsa.

Newspaper

*T*HE *first Catholic newspaper in Oklahoma was The Indian Advocate, published, first as a quarterly and then as a monthly, from 1888 to 1910. It was founded by Father Ignatius Jean, O.S.B., the second apostolic prefect of the Indian Territory, and it was published at Sacred Heart Abbey. From 1912 to 1921 The Orphans' Record was published as a monthly from St. Joseph's Orphanage. Beginning in 1922 Father Bernard Brotons, O.C.D., produced The Catholic Home, first at Hartshorne and then at Oklahoma City. In 1924 Bishop Kelley changed its name to the The Southwest Courier and took over as publisher. As editor he named Joseph Quinn, who had worked for Father Brotons, and who continued as editor until his retirement in 1960. That year Father John Joyce became editor; he and Jack Bickham restyled the paper in format and content as The Oklahoma Courier. The Courier ceased publication in 1969. In 1974, after a five-year hiatus, Archbishop Quinn directed Father David Monahan to begin a new archdiocesan publication, The Sooner Catholic, which continues to be the official newspaper of the Archdiocese of Oklahoma City.*

Archbishop Quinn

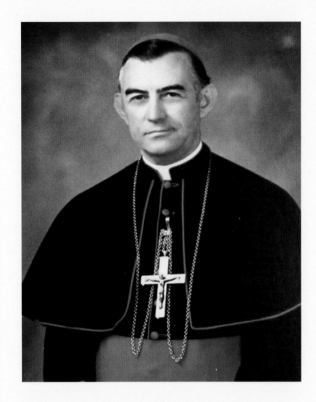

*S*INCE 1926 Catholic Oklahoma had belonged to the ecclesiastical province of San Antonio, Texas, whose archbishop in 1971 was Francis J. Furey, until recently the bishop of San Diego, California. His auxiliary and protégé there was the young Bishop John Raphael Quinn. It was no surprise to anyone in California when the first episcopal appointment in Archbishop Furey's province turned out to be that of Bishop Quinn as Oklahoma's fifth ordinary.

John Quinn was born in Riverside, California, a suburb of San Diego, on May 28, 1929. A brilliant student, he was sent for priestly studies to the North American College in Rome, where he was ordained a priest on July 19, 1953. Back in the United States, he was soon a professor, and then the rector, of San Diego's junior seminary. In 1967 he was appointed auxiliary bishop, ordained in San Diego on December 12, 1967. On January 5, 1972, he was installed

✦ After Mass in their parish church, these children are glad to greet Archbishop Quinn.

in Oklahoma City. He was then 42, and the youngest head of a diocese in the U.S.

At the time of his death, Bishop Reed was working on the long-awaited division of Oklahoma into two Catholic dioceses. Bishop Quinn carried this forward, with the result that on December 19, 1972, Rome announced that not only would the division take place, but that Oklahoma City would become an archdiocese with Quinn as its first archbishop. The ceremonies took place in Oklahoma City on February 6, 1973, with corresponding rites in Tulsa the following day.

As bishop and then archbishop, John Quinn's tenure was notable in several ways. First, he dealt with the increasing demands on the chancery office by moving the facility out of the archbishop's home and into a former insurance agency's building on Classen Boulevard. The diocesan newspaper had failed in the overheated church politics of the late 1960's; under Quinn's direction, The Oklahoma Courier was revived as The Sooner Catholic and received a new lease on life. He dealt creatively with problems caused by experimental, non-territorial parishes by having a respected Catholic polling agency, the Center for Applied Research in the Apostolate, in Washington, D.C., conduct a study which found that the parishes were not meeting their stated goals, thus leaving them open to termination. Of course, the division of the diocese meant a long series of civil and financial negotiations which were very time consuming. He won the respect of the leaders of other denominations, who elected him president of the Oklahoma Council of Churches.

In 1977 he was appointed archbishop of San Francisco and became, as he put it, "the first bishop to leave Oklahoma alive." Subsequently he served a 3-year term as president of the National Conference of Catholic Bishops of the United States, and he was the chair of that body's important theological committee, in which capacity he was involved in several crises involving American dioceses, religious orders of women, and Roman officials. He retired from San Francisco's archbishopric in 1995. He currently lives in San Francisco.

Archbishop Salatka

He started a planning process that led to a list of diocesan priorities (family life, youth ministry, and ministry to Hispanics were the first three out of eleven) and the sale of disposable property, as well as the consolidation of offices at the Archdiocesan Pastoral Center. He stressed the importance of welcoming ministry to Hispanics. He learned to read and speak Spanish at the age of 60. In accord with his episcopal motto, "Come Holy Spirit," he emphasized spiritual life for all the people of the diocese; the successful RENEW program was one result. He supported Catholic schools, insisted on the improvement of religious education, and cooperated in programs of adult Christian education, especially the Pastoral Ministry Program.

He instituted numerous programs to improve the quality of priestly service and took personal interest and insisted on the best of care when priests suffered health problems especially alcoholism. He supervised a building boom: at least thirteen new churches were built and major building efforts took place in eight other parishes. A new St. Ann's Nursing Home was constructed, and the former seminary was renovated into the Archdiocesan Pastoral Center (now called the Catholic Pastoral Center).

He practiced prudent stewardship over archdiocesan assets. With the help of a business advisory committee which he instituted, he saw the endowment fund of the archdiocese increase from $1,377,961 in 1977 to $22,566,387 in 1992. Total liquid assets at the time of his retirement were approximately $32,000,000.

*C*HARLES *Alexander Salatka, of Lithuanian-American descent, was born February 26, 1918, in Grand Rapids, Michigan. He was ordained for the diocese of Grand Rapids on February 24, 1945. After graduate studies in Europe, several pastorates, and assignments in the Grand Rapids chancery, he was appointed in 1961 as auxiliary bishop of the diocese. His episcopal ordination took place there on March 6, 1962.*

He was named ninth bishop of Marquette, on Michigan's Upper Peninsula, in January 1968, and his appointment as second archbishop of Oklahoma City was announced on September 27, 1977. He was installed in Oklahoma City on December 15.

His accomplishments as leader of the Catholic Church in western and central Oklahoma were numerous.

As a newly-ordained bishop, he attended all four sessions of the Second Vatican Council. When he resigned in 1991, Archbishop Salatka was the senior bishop, in terms of ordination, in the United States. He was then one of only a few active American bishops who had taken part in Vatican II. After a dozen years in retirement, he died, at the age of 86, on March 17, 2003.

❖ A scene repeated many times in and around Oklahoma City during the 1980's: Archbishop Salatka greets a parishioner.

Archbishop Beltran

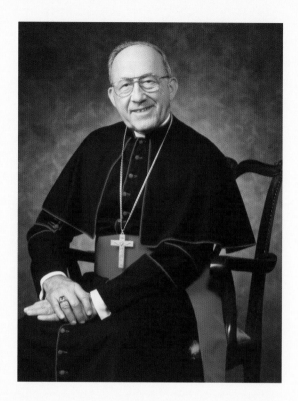

After studies at St. Charles Seminary in Overbrook, Pennsylvania, Father Eusebius Beltran was ordained a priest on May 14, 1960. His rise in Atlanta was swift; he was immediately chosen to work part-time in the chancery, and by 1963 he was vice-chancellor and head of the archdiocesan marriage tribunal. He accompanied Archbishop Paul Hallinan to the sessions of Vatican II as a peritus, or advisor. From 1971 to 1978 he was the vicar general of the Atlanta archdiocese. In addition he served as pastor at two parishes. The first was in the Atlanta suburbs; he gave this up to take on responsibility for an inner-city black parish.

His appointment as the second bishop of Tulsa was announced on February 28, 1978, and he was ordained at Holy Family Cathedral, Tulsa, on April 20 of that year. During his fifteen years in Tulsa, he became known for his concern for Catholic Charities, for Catholic schools, and for vocations to the priesthood. In each of these areas he developed innovative programs and extended the Church's reach throughout eastern Oklahoma.

THE fifth of nine children, Eusebius Joseph Beltran was born in Ashley, Pennsylvania, on August 31, 1934. He was given the name of his Spanish grandfather, a common name in Spain; several saints, one of them a pope, were named Eusebius. The archbishop's father, Joseph Beltran, was born in Spain and came to New York in his late teens; he traveled to Pennsylvania to get a job in the coal mines. Helen Rita Kozlowski, the archbishop's mother was born in the United States, though her parents were natives of Poland. In the early 1950's Joseph became ill with black lung disease. The doctors encouraged the family to move to the Southeast or the Southwest, so they moved to Gainesville, Georgia, in 1954. Two sons became priests, Joseph in 1955 and Eusebius in 1960, both for the archdiocese of Atlanta.

These same concerns have continued to guide his time in Oklahoma City. On November 24, 1992, it was announced that he had been appointed to succeed Archbishop Salatka as Oklahoma City's third archbishop. His installation took place on January 22, 1993; the ceremony was held in the Oklahoma City's Music Center auditorium because Our Lady's Cathedral could not hold all those who were expected to attend. Later the same year, he was summoned to Rome to receive the pallium, the sign of an archbishop's office, from the hands of Pope John Paul II; this took place in St. Peter's Basilica on June 29, 1993, the feast of Saints Peter and Paul.

✧ In Our Lady's Cathedral in Oklahoma City, Archbishop Beltran lays hands on Reverend Kirk Larkin during his ordination to the priesthood.

Center of Family Love

*I*N 1974 Joe Pierce had a dream: to build a home, under Catholic auspices, for the mentally disabled. The next year he and Harold Wittrock took the idea to the state convention of the Knights of Columbus, who commissioned them to investigate the project further and report back. In 1976 the Knights unanimously approved their proposal, and immediately raised $30,000 to get it moving. The next five years were spent raising the first $1,500,000 needed to build the facility. Money came in from foundations, from community drives, and from private individuals; they even received fifty cents from someone's babysitting money.

Banker Joe Loosen of Okarche donated twenty acres, and the citizens backed up his gift with over $300,000 in donations. With that kind of support, it was easy to see where the Center of Family Love would be built. Groundbreaking was in 1980, and by September 1981 the Center was ready for its first residents. The campus had an administration building, two dormitories, and soon, a workshop and a greenhouse. A wood shop opened in a former Kingfisher church. By 1985 the Center was beginning to place residents in community employment. In 1988 a $10,000 foundation grant enabled the Center to add commercial laundry equipment. That year the Center entered into its first supported employment contract with the state Department of Human Services. Ancillary group homes opened in Kingfisher and Yukon.

Today the Center provides employment training for more than 150 residents in all its programs. An annual Knights of Columbus statewide Tootsie Roll Drive raises over $45,000 in support of the Center.

Saint Ann Retirement Center

*S*T. ANN'S HOME, a housing center for the elderly, erected under the auspices of Catholic Charities, opened at 23rd and Portland Avenue in Oklahoma City in 1950. On January 24, 1992, Archbishop Salatka dedicated

St. Ann Nursing Home for convalescent and aged patients. This facility is located on property that was originally part of St. Francis DeSales Seminary (later the Center for Christian Renewal and now the Catholic Pastoral Center) in northwest Oklahoma City.

Adjacent to St. Ann Nursing Home is the latest addition to the Church's ministry to senior adults, the Saint Ann Retirement Center, an independent and assisted living facility that opened on April 20, 2002. St. Ann Nursing Home and Saint Ann Retirement Center are operated directly by the Archdiocese of Oklahoma City, independently of Catholic Charities.

When the nursing home was opened, the original St. Ann's Home was closed and converted into low-income housing for the elderly. It is now known as Villa Isenbart, in honor of the longtime director of Catholic Charities who built it.

Catholic Charities

IN 1912 Bishop Meerschaert fulfilled a cherished dream when he opened the new St. Joseph's Orphanage near Bethany. This was the first diocesan-based institution of charity in Oklahoma. The first superintendent was Father John Kekeisen, who built the first unit of the orphanage and served until his untimely death in 1919. He was followed by Father Peter Paul Schaefer, who was director until 1926.

In that year Bishop Kelley appointed Father James Garvey as director, not only of St. Joseph's but of a new institution called Catholic Charities. Over the years that followed, the St. Joseph's campus expanded with new programs and additional buildings. Especially notable were a residential program for elderly persons and Our Lady of Victory Maternity Home. Monsignor Garvey operated Catholic Charities until his death in 1949, when he was succeeded by Monsignor A.A. Isenbart.

Monsignor Isenbart was responsible for the original St. Ann's Home at 23rd and Portland, Oklahoma City, in 1950, along with other programs for groups of persons in need. In 1951 a separate office was opened in Tulsa, and the combined institution adopted the name Associated Catholic Charities. Demographic and philosophical changes among American agencies led to new approaches to Catholic Charities' mission. Today Catholic Charities of the Archdiocese of Oklahoma City has almost no

buildings, though it sponsors and operates a great number of agencies and programs. For example, as a result of the 1986 Immigration Reform and Control Act, the agency created an immigration program that has served thousands of persons seeking permanent residence in the United States; it is also very involved in the resettlement of refugees of many different backgrounds. To serve families in need of counseling, Catholic Charities began the St. Joseph Counseling Center in 1990; it offers therapy in all Catholic Charities service centers, in Oklahoma City, Lawton, Enid and Clinton.

In 1992 Catholic Charities started a ministry to persons with HIV or AIDS. In 1995 this was expanded with the opening of Elizabeth House, a transitional living center for such persons. Also in 1995 the Holy Family Maternity Home opened; this is a living center for pregnant and homeless teenage women. In 2001 Seton House opened as an independent living apartment complex for teenage homeless women and their children.

Catholic Charities sponsors two housing projects for low-income elderly persons, Villa Isenbart and Trinity Gardens, both opened in 1996. 1996 also saw development of three new programs: The SHARE (Self Help and Resource Exchange) program provides low cost groceries once a month to those who give two hours of service to the community; there are about fifty distribution sites throughout the archdiocese. The Family HOPE program is built on the social service care management theory and builds strong partnerships with families in need so they may achieve self-sufficiency. The Parish Nurse program uses registered professional nurses as part of a parish's ministry to offer health education, referral, and spiritual services.

In addition, Catholic Charities has programs in the following areas: adoption and foster care, teen parenting education, social action advocacy, disaster response, senior adult ministry, and parish development.

Our Lady of Guadalupe Catholic Youth Camp

On MAY 1, 2003, Archbishop Beltran celebrated his silver anniversary as a bishop. The homilist at the Mass of Thanksgiving, a seminary classmate, recalled how the young Father Eusebius Beltran enjoyed working at the summer camp sessions sponsored by his diocese, and how convinced he was of the importance of such camps in making the Catholic Faith real and alive for young people.

It should have come as no surprise, then, that the archbishop has continued in that conviction and that he has staunchly supported the idea of a Catholic summer camp during his years as a priest and bishop.

Even before the creation of a separate Oklahoma City archdiocese, Catholic boys and girls from all over western and central Oklahoma gathered for a series of week-long summer camp sessions each year. Throughout the 1980's and 1990's, these sessions were held at Lake Murray in Carter County, but this venue began disintegrating from age and lack of maintenance. Upon discovering that a tract of 320 acres was available in the Wellston area, the archbishop purchased it and set about planning the camp. The $1.5 million project was financed from Archdiocesan Development Fund monies over a three-year period. Construction began in 1999, and the camp, named for Our Lady of Guadalupe, was dedicated on May 21, 2000.

A series of log cabin dormitories, each with its own tornado safe room; a dining hall; a large swimming pool; five stocked fishing ponds; and several sports fields surround the camp's center, its chapel. To judge by the interest in the camp on the part of Catholic groups and others as well, the camp has a bright future.

Religious Women

*T*HE first women religious to work in Oklahoma were Benedictines from New Orleans who came to teach at St. Mary's Academy at Sacred Heart. They were here from 1880 to 1884. Other communities that followed include:

SISTERS OF MERCY

Five sisters came from a convent at Lacon, Illinois, arriving at St. Mary's Academy in 1884. The initial community grew quickly. After the fire that destroyed Sacred Heart in 1901, the sisters relocated their motherhouse to Mount St. Mary's in Oklahoma City, which opened in 1904. For almost half a century they were an independent community, but in 1929 they participated with other convents in creating the Sisters of Mercy of the Union, which has its center in St. Louis, Missouri. In Oklahoma they have been educators and hospital administrators.

BENEDICTINE SISTERS OF THE SACRED HEARTS OF JESUS AND MARY

Barely five months after the 1889 Land Run, three Benedictine sisters from a convent in Creston, Iowa, stepped from the train at the Guthrie station. They had been recruited to teach at St. Mary's School in the capital of the Oklahoma Territory.

In 1892 the remaining sisters, including Mother Mary Paula O'Reilly, O.S.B., the superior, moved from Iowa to a new building just west of Guthrie, St. Joseph's Academy and Motherhouse. From this center they staffed schools and other institutions all over the state, including Benedictine Heights Hospital in Guthrie, and schools at Langston, Okarche, Okeene, Kingfisher, Newkirk, Blackwell, and Duncan, part of a total of some fifty schools, hospitals, and orphanages throughout the state. They staffed St. Joseph's Orphanage in Oklahoma City (1933-44) and ran a night school for African Americans, Claver College, in Guthrie. In 1955 they transferred their motherhouse to Tulsa.

Their superior, Mother Mary Paula O'Reilly, O.S.B., was the heiress to a coal-mining fortune in Pennsylvania, and she made possible a two-story frame convent next door to the church. Two years later, the newly-consecrated Bishop Theophile Meerschaert would make this same building his own headquarters when he came to Guthrie from Natchez, Mississippi.

SISTERS OF BENEDICT

In 1968, 33 Benedictine sisters from St. Joseph's Monastery in Tulsa formed a new community, the Sisters of Benedict. The Sisters of Benedict was formally approved as an independent priory on February 18, 1970. In 1974, to fulfill a Benedictine tradition of having only one foundation in a diocese, the Sisters of Benedict located at Red Plains Priory next door to Our Lady's Cathedral in Oklahoma City, In 1996 they moved to a new convent at Piedmont, northwest of Oklahoma City, where they offer retreats, spiritual direction, workshops, Taize and labyrinth prayer experiences, lectio divina and centering prayer, and a seven-month experience called Retreat in Daily Life, as well as a five-year process for training spiritual directors.

SISTERS OF ST. FRANCIS OF PHILADELPHIA

Catherine Drexel began supporting mission schools even before she founded her own religious order. To staff these, she called on a Franciscan community of sisters founded in Philadelphia in 1855. Comprised mostly of German and Irish women, this community originally was intended to assist immigrants arriving in the city. Though they were not trained as teachers, the Franciscans accepted the challenge of staffing several schools in Oklahoma. Their missions within the present archdiocese included St. Elizabeth's in Purcell, St. Patrick's in Anadarko, and St. Joseph's in Chickasha.

FRANCISCAN SISTERS OF MARY, ST. LOUIS, MISSOURI

Two Franciscan Sisters from Maryville, Missouri opened the first hospital in the Oklahoma Territory, St. Anthony's in Oklahoma City, in 1898. In 1964 the Franciscans took over the operation of Benedictine Heights Hospital in Guthrie, running it as Alverno Heights Hospital until 1972. In 1987 the Franciscan Sisters of Maryville amalgamated with the Sisters of St. Mary of the Third Order of St. Francis to become the Franciscan Sisters of Mary in St. Louis, Missouri.

SISTERS OF DIVINE PROVIDENCE

This community was formed in Alsace-Lorraine and transferred to Texas in the 1870's. Its motherhouse is in San Antonio. Since their first school in Perry in 1900, more than 850 members of the community have taught in Oklahoma parochial schools.

ADORERS OF THE BLOOD OF CHRIST

Formerly known as the Sisters Adorers of the Most Precious Blood, these sisters, based in Wichita, Kansas, simplified their name in 1968. They have provided Oklahomans an unusual array of services, from teaching and nursing to domestic work, with several ministries often carried out in the same mission.

CARMELITE SISTERS OF ST. THERESE

Founded in 1917 at Bentley, Atoka County, Oklahoma, this community is one of the few sisterhoods ever originated in our state. Principal figures in the Carmelites' history are Father Edward Soler, O.C.D., the founder, and Sister Agnes Marie Cavanaugh, C.S.T., superior general from 1928 to 1951. The community received canonical status from Rome in 1928; since then the sisters have staffed more than thirty missions throughout Oklahoma. The present motherhouse, Villa Teresa in Oklahoma City, was established in 1933.

CARMEL OF ST. JOSEPH

At the invitation of Bishop Kelley and through the mediation of Carmelite Father Vincent Martinez, Mother Teresa Cawley and her niece, Sister Stephen Kane, came to Oklahoma in 1939 from the Discalced Carmelites of the Bronx, New York. They were followed by four more nuns in 1940. A strictly contemplative, cloistered community, the nuns bake most of the Communion hosts used in churches throughout Oklahoma and other parts of the country. Their motherhouse is now located in Piedmont, Oklahoma.

SISTERS OF ST. JOSEPH OF WICHITA

This community traces its origins to France around 1650. The first American foundation was made at Carondelet, Missouri, in 1836. In 1883 Sisters of St. Joseph came to Leavenworth, Kansas, from whence they established an independent house at Abilene, Kansas. A series of diocesan boundary changes brought the Abilene community within the diocese of Wichita, where they were established in 1900. Since 1921 the community has sponsored the St. Joseph Regional Medical Center of Northern Oklahoma, Inc., at Ponca City, along with several schools and other institutions.

Catholic Women

WOMEN HOMESTEADERS

Between roughly 1880 and 1910, Catholic homesteads on the Oklahoma frontier surely owed their perseverance in faith, in large part, to women. Catholic wives and mothers and community leaders had their work cut out for them in population centers that were characterized by a vanishing way of life among the Indian villages, early farms scattered on the desolate and treeless plains, towns just beginning to grow in the wake of railroad development and land runs, and the rowdy camps of oil field workers. But, for the most part, this important work was unheralded and unrecorded.

CATHOLIC TEACHING SISTERS

Somewhat better remembered is the work of the Catholic teaching sisters in Oklahoma, especially among the Benedictines, Sisters of Mercy, and Carmelites of St. Therese.

❖ CARMELITES OF ST. THERESE

Mother Agnes Teresa Cavanaugh, C.S.T. (1894-1951)

Mother Agnes Teresa Cavanaugh is considered the foundress of the Carmelite Sisters of St. Therese. As Marie Loretta Cavanaugh, she came from Rhode Island to rural Oklahoma at the request of Father Edward Soler, O.C.D., to teach school to the Choctaw congregation of St. Henry's parish in Bentley, Atoka County. In time she and two companions began to wear the Carmelite habit, and in 1917 she was professed as the first member of a new religious community. Canonical approval was obtained in 1928, at which time she was elected superior general, a post she held until her death in 1951.

❖ BENEDICTINES

The Benedictine Sisters of Guthrie and Tulsa produced many remarkably talented and creative women who gave themselves to the service of the Oklahoma Church. To single out any of them seems remiss to the others, but to the historian, two names do stand out.

Mother Mary Paula O'Reilly, O.S.B. (1839-1921)

Mother Mary Paula O'Reilly, the community's founder and first superior, was born in Pennsylvania. She was the heiress to a coal mining fortune, which she made available to her community to fund their early activities, especially construction of the St. Joseph Academy and Motherhouse west of Guthrie. She made the decision to move the sisters from their convent at Creston, Iowa, to the Oklahoma Territory in 1892. She was the superior until 1900, when tensions within the group caused her to move to Atchison, Kansas, where she died.

Sister Mary Charles Bryce, O.S.B. (1916-2002)

Sister Mary Charles Bryce was born in Ramona, Oklahoma, of Cherokee-Choctaw heritage. She made her perpetual vows at Guthrie in 1943, and transferred to the Sisters of Benedict in 1968. In 1960 she earned a master's degree in religious education at The Catholic University of America in Washington, D.C.

In 1964 she received a full-time faculty appointment in religious studies, the first time a woman had been appointed to such a post in this country. She gained initial notoriety with the publication of a first-communion instruction book that did not include the prior necessity of confession. She had, however, the firm support ●●●

●●● *of her bishop, Victor J. Reed, who assured her that the book was both good and helpful. At Catholic University she was a major influence, insisting that the department of religion and religious education, as it had now become, continue to emphasize liturgy and sacramental catechesis. She promoted the cause of women, especially sisters, in higher education, and she wrote about pioneer women in catechetics. Her 1971 doctoral dissertation examined how the Baltimore Catechism shaped the content of catechetical materials in the U.S.*

In 1984 she published Pride of Place: The Role of the Bishop in the Development of Catechesis in the United States. The same year she accepted the Flannery Chair of Theology in the School of Religious Studies at Gonzaga University, Spokane, Washington.

❖ SISTERS OF MERCY

Sister Mary Francis Troy, R.S.M. (1862-1939)

Sister Mary Francis Troy, R.S.M., who was professed at Sacred Heart in 1886, served many years as superior of the community's flagship institution, Mt. St. Mary's Academy in Oklahoma City. In 1935 she was named to the Oklahoma Hall of Fame.

Sister Mary Coletta Massoth, R.S.M. (1919-1983)

Sister Mary Coletta Massoth, a native of Piqua, Kansas, was professed in the Sisters of Mercy of the Union in 1942. She became well-known for her leadership of the sisters in Oklahoma at the time a decision had to be made as to the relocation of Mercy Hospital in Oklahoma City. *Although building a new hospital on the far north of the city seemed impractical and was hotly controverted, Sister Mary Coletta saw the entire project through in spite of*

many difficulties. The new Mercy Hospital was dedicated in 1974. Her brother, Father Charles Massoth, O.S.B., is a former abbot of St. Gregory's in Shawnee.

❖ EXTENSION LAY VOLUNTEERS

This lay organization was formed in Oklahoma by Father John Sullivan, pastor of Guthrie. Father Sullivan developed the idea of recruiting Catholic college students to devote two years after graduation as teachers in parochial schools, as nurses in Catholic hospitals, or as parish workers in rural communities. This idea was picked up by the Catholic Church Extension Society in 1960, and Father Sullivan went to Chicago to serve as its national director. The Extension Lay Volunteers, unfortunately, became a victim of the political and religious convulsions of the 1960's, and the program had to be suspended in 1968.

❖ SHIRLEY COX

Shirley Cox (1950-), an author, lecturer, corporate lawyer, and psychiatric social worker, has worked for Catholic Charities of Oklahoma City since 1987. For ten years she developed and directed Catholic Charities' immigration assistance program, becoming in the process a local and regional speaker on immigration issues. At present she is the director of the social action program at Catholic Charities, serving as the archdiocese's public policy advocate on such issues as welfare reform, the elderly, pro-life, death penalty, corrections, immigration, and poverty. In this capacity she is also the liaison between Archbishop Beltran and the Oklahoma State Legislature.

❖ SISTER MARTHA MARY McGAW, C.S.J.

Sister Martha Mary McGaw (1915-1995) served as co-editor of The Sooner Catholic from 1978 to 1995. During those years the Catholic Press Association at its annual meetings gave her no less than nineteen awards.

Sister Martha Mary came to her career in journalism later than most. She taught for 34 years at the elementary, secondary, and collegiate levels before turning to 25 years of work as a writer and photographer.

She was the author of Stevenson in Hawaii, reprinted in 1978, and a popular paperback, 60 Ways to Let Yourself Grow. Among her interview subjects for The Sooner Catholic were cartoonist Charles Schultz, theologian Avery Dulles, aerospace pioneer Chuck Yeager, and Harvard University's George Hunston Williams. Before coming to Oklahoma, she interviewed and photographed Ansel Adams, himself a world-famous photographer. When he saw her photo of him, Adams was so impressed he asked for the negative.

❖ INDIAN BALLERINAS

Among the famous Oklahoma ballerinas from Indian tribes are Catholics Maria and Marjorie Tallchief (Osage), and Yvonne Chouteau. Yvonne Chouteau (1929-), of Cherokee, Creek, and French heritage, is a veteran (1943-61) of the Ballet Russe de Monte Carlo, the youngest American ever to dance there. She held the title of prima ballerina at the Ballet Russe for eight years. A former artist-in-residence at the University of Oklahoma, she also played an active role in her parish's liturgy committee in Oklahoma City. All three of these women have been named to the Oklahoma Hall of Fame, as well as many state, national, and international honors.

❖ LUCILLE MULHALL

In a very different area of entertainment, Lucille Mulhall (1884-1940) was a world champion rodeo star, the only woman who ever roped steers competitively with men. Practically born in the saddle, she traveled with her father's Wild West show and in vaudeville for some twenty years. New York newspapers, attempting to explain her phenomenon, invented the term "cowgirl" to describe her.

❖ KATE BARNARD

Perhaps the most important Catholic woman in Oklahoma history was Kate Barnard (1875-1930). Born in Nebraska, but an Oklahoman from the age of 12, she was

elected state commissioner of charities and corrections in 1907, becoming the first American woman ever elected to statewide office.

She was a key figure in the enactment of a compulsory education law with provision of state payments to widows dependent on their children's earnings, of legislation implementing the constitutional ban on child labor, and of laws aimed at unsafe working conditions and the blacklisting of union men. Appalled by conditions when touring a prison where Indian Territory prisoners were housed, she undertook the design and construction of the Oklahoma State Penitentiary at McAlester in 1909, at the time a state-of-the-art facility.

❖ LOUTITIA DENISON EASON

Wife, mother, and attorney, Loutitia Eason was appointed vice-chancellor of the Oklahoma City archdiocese in February 2004 and, following the retirement of her predecessor, chancellor in July 2004. She is the first lay person to hold the post in the archdiocese. She received her doctorate from the University of Oklahoma College of Law and was admitted to the bar in 1979. Mrs. Eason was general counsel for the Oklahoma department of securities before entering private practice, where she concentrated in business law, public trust law, and matters involving religious and nonprofit bodies. Her special interest as a professional and as a volunteer is working with entities that provide affordable housing; she has served on the boards of Villa Isenbart and Trinity Gardens, both projects for the elderly developed by Catholic Charities. She has lectured on housing issues facing the elderly and has volunteered for Habitat for Humanity. She is a member of the Laughlin House Committee, a project of St. Eugene parish in Oklahoma City that provides transitional housing to families in need. Mrs. Eason is a member of the archdiocesan social justice commission.

7 Parishes

✧ This stained-glass window is from Saint Mary Church in Medford.

Former Churches

*I*N Oklahoma today, more than 850 settlements are classified as "ghost towns," places that formerly flourished but which were made redundant by economic or other changes. This is reflected in the number of Catholic parishes that no longer exist. In 1924, for the first time, the greater part of the U.S. population lived in cities, whereas previously the nation had been mostly rural.

❖ ALVARETTA (Woods),
  St. Wenceslaus (1903-1912)
❖ ANVIL (Lincoln),
  St. Michael (1893-1904)
❖ ANTHON (Custer),
  Ss. Peter and Paul (1901-1962)
❖ CAPRON (Woods),
  Immaculate Conception (1901-1916)
❖ CANUTE (Washita),
  Holy Family (1926-1970)
❖ CARMEN (Alfalfa),
  Sacred Heart (1918-1931)
❖ CHATANOOGA (Comanche),
  St. Patrick (1909-1932)
❖ CHEYENNE (Roger Mills),
  St. Joseph (1924-1976)
❖ CLYDE (Grant),
  St. Anthony (1898-1963)
❖ CONCEPTION (Oklahoma),
  Immaculate Conception (1892-1930)
❖ CORN (Washita),
  Immaculate Conception (1897-1904)
❖ CYRIL (Caddo),
  Immaculate Conception (1928-1978)
❖ EASON/Trousdale (Pottawatomie),
  St. Gregory (1907-1925)
❖ ENID (Garfield),
  St. Elizabeth (1946-1959)
❖ GEARY (Blaine),
  St. Joseph (1902-1977)
❖ GOOD SHEPHERD (Cimarron),
  Good Shepherd (1893-1908)
❖ GUTHRIE (Logan),
  St. Catherine (1894-1933, 1947-1970)
❖ HENNESSEY (Kingfisher),
  Holy Rosary (1902-1941)
❖ KOLLMAN (Beaver),
  St. Peter (1915-1954)
❖ HITCHCOCK (Blaine),
  St. Francis, Sacred Heart (1911-1997)
❖ HUNTER (Garfield),
  St. Anthony (1928-1937)
❖ HYDRO (Caddo),
  Blessed Virgin (1904-1965)
❖ INDEPENDENCE/ANTHONY (Custer),
  Ss. Peter and Paul (1901-1908)
❖ KEOKUK FALLS (Pottawatomie),
  St. Wenceslaus (1898-1906)
❖ LANGSTON (Logan),
  Holy Family (1893-1920, 1948-1977)
❖ LEXINGTON (Cleveland),
  St. John the Baptist (1890-1999)
❖ LOCKRIDGE (Logan),
  St. Patrick (1891-1960)

❖ LOYAL (Kingfisher),
  St. Francis Xavier, St. Joseph (1900-1997)
❖ LUTHER (Oklahoma),
  St. Peter Claver, St. Theresa of the Infant Jesus (1899-2000)
❖ MANCHESTER (Grant),
  Ss. Peter and Paul (1898-1955)
❖ MINCO (Grady),
  Our Lady of the Holy Rosary (1893-1918)
❖ MISHAK (Oklahoma),
  St. Martin (1909-1911, 1914-1931)
❖ MULHALL (Logan),
  St. Agnes, St. Margaret (1892-1921, 1953-1967)
❖ NAVINA (Logan),
  Sacred Heart (1913-1983)
❖ NUMA (Grant),
  St. Mary (1898-1940)
❖ OKLAHOMA CITY (Oklahoma),
  Assumption of Mary (1954-1963)
❖ OKLAHOMA CITY (Oklahoma),
  Community of John XXIII (1966-1975)
❖ OKLAHOMA CITY (Oklahoma),
  Immaculate Heart of Mary (1952-1963)
❖ OKLAHOMA CITY (Oklahoma),
  St. Peter Claver (1925-1964)
❖ PECKHAM (Kay),
  St. Patrick (1906-1919)
❖ PLEASANT VALLEY (Logan),
  Sacred Heart (1910-1921)
❖ QUINLAN (Woodward),
  Sacred Heart (1917-1934)
❖ RINGWOOD (Major),
  St. Ethlebert (1952-1968)
❖ ROOSEVELT (Kiowa),
  Holy Family (1916-1939)
❖ SCHEIDEL (Washita),
  St. Francis of Assisi (1900-1970)
❖ SHAWNEETOWN (Lincoln),
  (1886-1892)
❖ SNYDER (Kiowa),
  St. Anthony (1908-1910)
❖ SPARKS (Lincoln),
  St. Cecilia (1905-1920)
❖ SUGDEN (Jefferson),
  San Jose (1974-1985)
❖ SYRIA (Woods),
  (1919-1931)
❖ TECUMSEH (Pottawatomie),
  Our Lady of the Holy Rosary (1894-1925)
❖ TEMPLE (Cotton),
  St. Mary of the Assumption (1910-1920)
❖ TIPTON,
  Sacred Heart (1961-2000)

The Unassigned Lands

I N 1834 Congress considered a bill that would have created a region called the Indian Territory, which would consist of all land between the Mississippi River and the Rocky Mountains that was not a state or territory at the time or in the future. The bill did not pass, but the idea of the Indian Territory took hold in the public imagination. By 1870 all that remained of Indian Territory was the present state of Oklahoma, minus the Panhandle.

During most of the 19th century, the official policy of the federal government with regard to Native Americans was removal, that is, resettling the various tribes from homelands that had become desirable to Anglo-Americans to areas of the country west of the Mississippi. Beginning in 1825 a large group, the Five Civilized Tribes, was transported to what today is Oklahoma. Between 1866 and 1885 further removals created numerous reservations in the future state. These were formed from the outer boundaries inward, so that by 1889 there was a tract of 1,800,000 acres in the midst of the reservations that was not assigned to any tribe.

In the 1880's the U.S. was in the grip of land fever, and soon Congress was being dunned on behalf of white settlement in the Unassigned Lands. In March 1889 lobbyists finally succeeded in attaching a rider to the annual Indian Appropriations Bill that declared the Unassigned Lands open for white settlement. In his executive order, President Benjamin Harrison declared that this provision would take effect at noon on the Monday after Easter, April 22, 1889.

What happened next was unexpected. Some 50,000 persons from every part of North America, Europe, and Australia began descending on the American Midwest, lining up on the boundaries of a huge tract that was completely undeveloped and unprepared to receive them. At the appointed hour federal troopers fired their rifles, and by nightfall six new towns stood where before there had been only barren prairie.

Within five months of the 1889 Land Run, there were three Catholic churches standing in the newly opened territory. By 2000, 66 Catholic parishes and institutions had flourished there at one time or other.

April 22 1889

•Guthrie

CRESCENT
St. Margaret Mary

THIS Logan County church was built as a project of Father John Sullivan, pastor of Guthrie from 1947 to 1959. St. Margaret Mary's opened in 1953. For years its pastor was Father George R. Carpentier, O.P. the saintly pastor of Guthrie's parish for African-American Catholics, St. Catherine's. Bishop McGuinness blessed the new St. Margaret Mary's on April 30, 1956. A week later the bishop received word from Catholic Extension that a donation of $25,000 had been granted. After Father Carpentier retired in 1965, the Crescent parish became the responsibility of priests teaching at Bishop McGuinness High School. In recent years it has been in the care of the pastor of St. Mary's in Guthrie.

DEL CITY ◈ *St. Paul the Apostle*

DEL CITY, with a current population of 36,000, was founded in 1946 by George Epperly, who purchased and developed 160 acres in what is now the center of town. At first known as Epperly Heights, Del City was eventually named for the developer's daughter, Delaphene Campbell. Similarly, St. Paul the Apostle parish was founded in 1956 as St. Francis Xavier. With Father Bernard Havlik as first pastor, it was planned to serve the people of Del City and southeast Oklahoma City.

By 1966 the parish had grown to 340 families, and there was a need for a larger church. The parish bought ten acres on Sunnylane Road, and ground was broken for a new building in January 1966. The first Mass in the new church was celebrated on October 2, 1966, and Bishop Reed dedicated it on November 22. The parish name change occurred in 1967, apparently at the instigation of then-pastor Father Ernest Flusche. In 1979 a new parish rectory was built adjacent to the church, and a parish hall was added in 1985. The parish now numbers about 450 families.

EDMOND ◈ *St. John the Baptist*

THE first Catholic church (and the first of any denomination) in the Oklahoma Territory was at Edmond, a coaling stop on the Santa Fe rail line halfway between Oklahoma Station and Guthrie. Catholic settlers in the new village challenged the other citizens that if everybody would contribute to their proposed project, they would put out an Associated Press dispatch saying that a church was already standing in the Territory. Credit was also due Father N. F. Scallan, who had arrived in the territory in May, just two weeks after the Land Rush.

The small but serviceable frame church, which cost about $500.00, was dedicated on June 24, 1889, the feast of St. John the Baptist. At first the church was served from Oklahoma City, and it was used by all the denominations until their own church houses were built. This kind of cooperation was characteristic of men and women in the raw new land, when religious prejudice was a luxury that few could afford. (The situation would not last, unfortunately.) A second church was built under the pastorate of Father John Metter, who attended Edmond from Norman. Bishop Meerschaert dedicated it in August 1900, but in March 1936 it was partly destroyed by fire.

At this point the parish bought property at its present location, Ninth and Littler, where the church was moved and rebuilt. It served through the remainder of the Depression and the war years. It was finally replaced by a brick church in 1955. This building still stands, though it is now used by the parish school.

Beginning in the 1970's, the parish undertook a series of building programs that transformed its campus. First came a new rectory, built in 1977. The fourth and present church, seating 825, was completed in 1982, during the pastorate of Father Marvin Leven. He added a two-story learning center in 1986, now home to St. Elizabeth Seton elementary school, which opened in 1990. The parish center, completed under Father John Petuskey in 1994, is a 28,000-square-foot structure housing a gymnasium, kitchen, commons, youth lounge, nursery, exercise and craft rooms, meeting rooms, and parish offices. The Kyle Douglas McMaster Library, at the south end of the Learning Center, comprises 3,800 square feet and was dedicated in 1996.

EDMOND
St. Monica

ST. JOHN THE BAPTIST church is the oldest Catholic parish in the region opened by the Run of 1889. It might seem odd that over a hundred years would pass before a second parish would be established there. In fact, however, another parish did exist in the area for many years; St. Patrick's (1891-1959), was situated at a settlement northwest of Edmond variously known as Kerry Corner, Deer Creek, and Lockridge —the last from the fact that it stood on a rise at the junction of four counties whose initials formed the word "lock".

On May 21, 1993, Archbishop Beltran announced that a new parish would be created on the west side of Edmond. He appointed Father Anthony Taylor as the first pastor. Father Taylor determined that a twenty-acre site just north of the Danforth Farms addition would be ideal for the parish complex. The archdiocese purchased the property in November 1993 as a gift to the new parish, and provided a loan for start-up expenses, including purchase of a house on adjoining land to serve as a rectory. The first parish office was established at the home of the volunteer parish secretary, Jeanne Ferguson.

Organizational meetings were held during the summer, at which parishioners voted to be a Total Stewardship parish; they also decided that the sequence of construction would begin with a parish center, followed by a church, school, gymnasium, and rectory. Three parish names were chosen and submitted to the archbishop, who chose St. Monica, mother of St. Augustine, as the parish titular. A provisional parish council was chosen. In September the altar society was organized and Council 11237 of the Knights of Columbus began in January 1994.

The first Masses were offered on the weekend of September 4-5, 1993, in the cafeteria of Washington Irving elementary school, at which Archbishop Beltran formally established the parish and blessed the new pastor. The events were attended by some 500 parishioners. In November services were moved to Santa Fe High School, as the parish already required more space. A rectory, a home in an adjacent housing addition, was purchased in 1993. Groundbreaking for the new parish center was held on December 5, construction began in January 1994, and the building was ready for occupancy when it was dedicated on September 23, 1994. Much ancillary work during construction was carried out by the parishioners themselves, including the laying of 60,000 square feet of sod. The final step in the development of the parish complex took place on July 14, 2000, when a new church was dedicated with a seating capacity of 1,000.

In May 2003, 833 families were registered at St. Monica's, and 535 students were enrolled in the religious education program. Because the parish practices total stewardship, there are no building drives or special fundraisers. Everything is financed directly from the weekly collection, to which all parishioners are expected to contribute five percent of their income.

EL RENO
Sacred Heart

EL RENO was among the first six towns to develop immediately after the 1889 Land Run, but its evolution was slow. Located just east of the 98th Meridian and a little below the North Canadian River, the townsite was also a few miles east of Fort Reno, an Army post established in 1874 named for Civil War General Jesse L. Reno.

The problem was in determining the best place for the town to be built. Several competing townsite companies made claims in the area, only to have floodwaters or mosquitoes argue against the virtues of their much-touted locations. Each of these places had its own name, variously Reno, Reno City, or the like. The site that finally won out became El Reno, emphatically *the* Reno.

Catholic mission activity began in 1890, and the first parish church arose two years later, no doubt reflecting the early confusion over placement of the townsite. One of the French Benedictines from Sacred Heart, 30-year-old Father Germanus Guillaume, was the first priest in the area. In 1887 he had been one of the first four priests ordained in the Indian Territory. He was pastor of El Reno until 1898, when he was replaced by another Benedictine, Father Constantine Pourcin. Father Constantine built the second church in 1902, and he also founded churches at Geary and Calumet.

By 1899 Sacred Heart parish had over 600 members, and in that year it opened its own school. There were ninety pupils the first year, with Sisters of Mercy (and later, Sisters of Divine Providence) as teachers. The school opened in an old storefront, with classrooms on the first floor and sisters' living quarters above.

The Knights of Columbus, a Catholic fraternal and mutual insurance organization, had begun in New Haven, Connecticut, in 1882. Within twenty years, it had grown throughout the United States, into Mexico, the Philippines, and every American state and territory—except one. In 1903, Council #767 was begun at El Reno, Oklahoma Territory, and the Knights' American hegemony was complete. In 1912 the organization was instrumental in having Columbus Day declared a state holiday. A new school was built that year in El Reno to house the 190 students then enrolled at Sacred Heart Academy.

The 1902 church was pulled down in 1950, but because of the Korean War, the replacement structure —the present church— was not fully erected in its place until 1951. Ten years later a new school was built but, like so many others in Oklahoma, it had to close in 1968. However, through the diligent work of many parishioners, a development committee was formed in 1997 and the new school building was dedicated by Archbishop Beltran on August 29, 1999, currently with PreK-6. When the parish observed its year-long centennial in 1990-91, it counted some 400 families as members.

GUTHRIE
St. Mary

Sisters from a small convent at Creston, Iowa, invited by the apostolic prefect, Father Ignatius Jean, O.S.B., to start a school in Guthrie, arrived by train on September 25, 1889. Thus began a ministry of Benedictine women in Oklahoma that has continued to the present day.

On September 19, 1891, the new Catholic bishop, Theophile Meerschaert, arrived in Guthrie to begin a 32-year pastorate in Oklahoma. For his residence, he appropriated a two-story convent that the Benedictine sisters had just built next door to St. Mary's. St. Mary's would be the site of Oklahoma's first parochial school, the first residence of an Oklahoma bishop, and the scene of the first ordination of a diocesan priest. (This was Father William Henry Ketcham, who would go on to become the director of the Bureau of Catholic Indian Missions, Washington, D.C., and a pivotal figure in the American Church's ministry to its native population.)

ST. MARY'S CHURCH in Guthrie was dedicated on September 8, 1889, the feast of the Birth of Mary. In President Harrison's order authorizing the Land Run, Guthrie and Kingfisher had been designated as places to register claims, and so right from the beginning Guthrie was a favored townsite. Like Edmond and Oklahoma Station, it was located on the Santa Fe right-of-way. Soon it would be designated the capital of the Oklahoma Territory, and for six years it would serve as the capital of the state of Oklahoma.

By the middle of June 1889, Father Felix DeGrasse, O.S.B., arrived from Pawhuska with orders from his Benedictine superior to assume pastoral responsibility for the northern part of the newly-opened region. Like most of his monastic brethren, Father Felix was a Frenchman, born in Bacourt in 1842 and ordained at Pierre-qui-Vire monastery in 1871. He had been in the Indian Territory since 1877; in fact, he had offered the first Mass at Sacred Heart Mission in May of that year. With over a dozen years of missionary experience, he was the logical choice for this pivotal appointment. Before long he would lay the groundwork for missions at Guthrie, Hennessey, Ponca City, and Perry, as well as other parishes that have since faded into oblivion.

His ministry in Guthrie was strongly influenced by two events that occurred within months of his own arrival. Three Benedictine

In 1905 Bishop Meerschaert moved his residence to the new cathedral city of Oklahoma City, and in 1910, in one of the rowdier episodes of Oklahoma political history, Guthrie lost the state capital, also to Oklahoma City. A new St. Mary's, the present church, was built in 1921. The bishop's residence next door was used as the parish rectory until it was replaced in the late 1950's. As Guthrie's black population developed on the west side, St. Catherine's parish was created to serve their needs. In addition, the Benedictine Sisters operated Claver College, a secondary-level school with evening classes, to help African-Americans in Guthrie further their education.

Father John J. Sullivan, pastor from 1947 to 1959, was responsible for a renaissance at St. Mary's. He built a new building for the parish school, which had closed in 1933. Father Sullivan also reopened St. Margaret's parish in Mulhall, which had closed in 1921; a new church was built there in 1953, which served the Catholics of that town until 1967. Father Sullivan also began recruiting young graduates from Catholic colleges to assist as teachers, nurses, and parish workers at St. Mary's and other institutions. This program soon developed into the lay volunteer program that was sponsored on a nationwide basis by Catholic Extension.

HENNESSEY
St. Joseph

FATHER Felix de Grasse, O.S.B., from the time he was assigned to Guthrie, was an extraordinarily active missionary to the region previously known as the Unassigned Lands, especially its northern part. Hennessey, some thirty miles northwest of Guthrie, was laid out on the Rock Island right-of-way on April 22, 1889. The railroad, building from the north, reached the new townsite in October, and a post office was established in April 1890. Beginning that year, Father Felix drove his buggy twice a month to Hennessey to say Mass. His "church" was the Rock Island section house, a building that housed railroad workers constructing that portion of the line as it snaked slowly southward from Kansas.

In the summer of 1891, Father Joseph Beck, then at Kingfisher, rented living space in the section house and picked up the missionary task at Hennessey. His first baptism took place on October 11, 1891. Anna Lola Redmund, from Downs, on the bank of the Cimarron River some ten miles south of Hennessey, was newly baptized that day. Father Beck was one of the five secular priests active in the Territory in this period (see page 12).

A year later, on November 13, 1892, Bishop Meerschaert presided at the dedication of St. Joseph's church in Hennessey. By this time the town had become a staging ground for the latest land openings. The reservation of the Cheyenne and Arapaho tribes, to the west, opened on April 19, 1892; and the massive Cherokee Outlet opened on September 16, 1893. But there was another cause for the population growth. A group of African-Americans, most of them from Kentucky, had taken up residence at Hennessey, and St. Joseph's was built for them. Money for the church came from Mother Katharine Drexel at the request of the bishop, who had traveled to her convent in Philadelphia to beg funds for missions for blacks and Native Americans. She donated a thousand dollars for the church, and this, combined with some smaller gifts, made possible construction of St. Joseph's between September and November 1892.

Father Beck continued as pastor of Hennessey until 1896, when progressive blindness forced his retirement.

During his pastorate he was active in starting other congregations in Union City and Pond Creek.

Given the state of race relations at the time, it is surprising that St. Joseph's managed to serve a mixed congregation, but apparently it did. In 1902, however, a second church, Holy Rosary, was built at the north end of town. Funding came from the Society for the Propagation for the Faith, then headquartered in Lyons, France. This became the black Catholics' church, and St. Joseph's reverted to the whites in the Catholic community. A parish school operated at St. Joseph's from 1921 to 1926; the building was later used as a parish hall.

Holy Rosary continued in use until 1941, by which time the black congregation had dwindled almost to nothing. In 1946 the building was jacked up and moved thirty miles north to Enid, where it became St. Elizabeth's chapel for black Catholics in that city.

After World War II, funds were raised for a new church, the present St. Joseph's, and Bishop McGuinness dedicated this on May 26, 1953. A new parish hall was constructed on the site of the old one in the early 1970's.

GUTHRIE
St. Catherine

would herself be canonized for her great love and care for African American and Native American children. In 1894, of course, she was still alive, was in fact still a young woman.

GUTHRIE'S second parish opened on its west side, the African American part of town, in 1894. The attending priest for nearly forty years was the chaplain of St. Joseph's Academy west of town, Father Placidus Diericks, O.S.B. Father Placidus was a major figure in the Church's apostolate to Oklahoma black Catholics before 1925. He also cared for Holy Family parish in Langston for some years. The Guthrie church was named in honor of St. Catherine—*which* St. Catherine was never made clear in the records—because this was an oblique way of honoring Mother Katharine Drexel, who

The parish closed in 1933, about the time that age and ill health caused Father Placidus to retire. Fourteen years later, however, it was revived because of the arrival in Oklahoma of another priest devoted to the black apostolate, the French Dominican Father George Carpentier (1887-1967). He came to Guthrie in 1946 to reestablish the parish. A new church was built the next year, and he served as pastor until he retired in 1965. A man of radical simplicity, who gave away anything that was given to him, he was reputed to be a saint in his own lifetime. In 1970 St. Catherine's was closed a second time.

KINGFISHER
Ss. Peter and Paul

ONE of the few structures standing in the Unassigned Lands on April 22, 1889, was a stagecoach station along the Chisholm Trail owned by a man named King Fisher. This served as a gathering point for pioneers entering the new region from the west. Two days before the Run, a post office was opened whose name was Lisbon, after an Ohio settler's hometown. In July 1889 the post office was renamed Kingfisher. Father Felix DeGrasse, the intrepid missionary-pastor of Guthrie, offered Mass in private homes at Kingfisher soon after the Run, and in 1892 the first church was built. Dedicated to St. Anne, it was constructed at the corner of Eighth and Wyatt under the supervision of Father Joseph Beck, the first resident pastor.

Father Frederick Vander Aa receives credit for beginning the second, and present, church, whose cornerstone was laid in 1903. Construction delays, including storm damage, meant that the church was not completed for several years. Ss. Peter and Paul Church, at Main and Euclid, was dedicated August 3, 1909. Situated directly on U.S. Highway 81, it has been a Kingfisher landmark for nearly a century. The parish school began in 1910; it moved to new quarters in 1928, and continues to serve the parish and town today. Father Theophile Van Hulse, the youngest of a trio of Belgian priest-brothers who came to the Oklahoma Territory in the 1890's, became pastor in 1928 and directed the Kingfisher parish until his retirement thirty years later.

A mission of Kingfisher was St. Joseph's at Loyal, some thirteen miles northwest. Loyal was founded as Kiel, after the German Baltic seaport, because many of the original settlers were from Germany. During World War I, however, anti-German sentiment caused the citizens of Kiel to rename their town Loyal. St. Joseph's was founded in 1898, but in 1997 its closing, like that of so many small rural parishes, occurred because of declining population and improved transportation to larger parishes.

MARSHALL
St. Camillus

FATHER Gustave Depreitere was Bishop Meerschaert's nephew. He was ordained in 1895 and arrived in Oklahoma the same year. He served at Hennessey and then at Enid, from whence in 1903 he organized the parish at Marshall, in northern Logan County. Under his direction the parishioners held a large picnic to raise funds for a church, which was built the same year.

Marshall's best-known citizen was the Oklahoma historian, Angie Debo. One of her many books, *Prairie City*, describes the evolution of daily life in rural Oklahoma from the years just after the 1889 Run until modern times. The model for her fictionalized memoir was, of course, her hometown. At one point, she describes the founding of the local Catholic church by a "Father Ledoux," including the picnic and the fact that as many non-Catholic townspeople as possible crowded into the

new church at its dedication, curious but unsure whether, if they were to kneel down, they might not be taking part in pagan rites.

Father Depreitere named the church in honor of the patron saint of his brother, Camille. Camille Depreitere's son, Emil, was the grand-nephew of Bishop Meerschaert. He, too, came to Oklahoma and was ordained for service here by his great-uncle in 1918.

From 1945 to 1970 Marshall was an independent parish. It is now a mission of Hennessey.

MOORE ◆ St. Andrew

BISHOP Reed set himself a personal goal of ensuring that a parish named for each of the twelve apostles would be erected in his statewide diocese. Toward that end, St. Andrew's was established as a mission of St. Joseph's in Norman. Bishop McGuinness had already approved the purchase of property in Moore, but he had died by the time 45 families began the new parish under the leadership of Father Joseph Duffy, pastor of St. Joseph's. Father Duffy himself died of cancer in 1962 while still in his thirties, and Father John Joyce assumed responsibility for the fledgling mission while maintaining his post as editor of the diocesan newspaper.

At first, Masses were held at Holy Child School, then operated by the Carmelite Sisters at a location between Norman and Moore. A rectory was built in 1963, and Father Joyce, who had been living at the seminary, took up residence in Moore. Church construction began in 1964, and the building opened the next year, to serve a parish that by then numbered 140 families. The first Mass there was offered in February 1965. Sizable additions, to accommodate an expanding religious education program, were added in 1972 and 1977; and a new church opened on the feast of St. Andrew, November 30, 1979. In 1980 the parish obtained property in Newcastle that now serves a family religious education program for Blanchard, Newcastle, and Tuttle. St. Andrew's staff has gradually increased to include full-or part-time personnel to serve in the areas of religious education, adult education, counseling, and youth ministry.

MIDWEST CITY ◆ *St. Philip Neri*

THE flurry of new parish development among Catholics in the Oklahoma City area that had begun with the arrival of Bishop Kelley in 1924 came to an abrupt halt after 1929, as the state and the nation settled into a long period of economic depression. On the heels of the Depression came the Second World War, with its stringent restrictions on all things, including construction materials, needed for the war effort. Not until 1946 did the former Unassigned Lands see another new parish created.

Midwest City was incorporated southeast of Oklahoma City in 1943; it took its name from the adjacent Midwest Air Depot (now Tinker Air Force Base). During the war years a small number of Catholics were served by the airfield chapel and the priests of Sacred Heart parish on Capitol Hill. Bishop Eugene McGuinness established a new parish on March 28, 1946, named it in honor of the 16th century Italian missionary St. Philip Neri, and appointed Father John T. Murray as pastor.

The first Mass in the parish was celebrated in a classroom at Jarman Junior High School. As the number of parishioners grew, the Mass was moved to the school's auditorium. Meanwhile, Father Murray searched for a permanent site, which he found on Felix Place, and which he purchased in March 1947 at a cost of $1,067. With help from the bishop and Catholic Extension, the first church was built for $14,250, and Mass was first offered there on August 3, 1947. This building would serve the parish, now numbering over a hundred families, for the next nine years.

A surplus chapel from the Navy base at Norman became available, and it was purchased to serve the growing parish. Cut into three pieces, it was transported over narrow roads to the parish site. The first church became the rectory, and the pastor no longer had to commute from his temporary residence at Sacred Heart.

St. Philip Neri school opened in 1954 with eight classrooms and a large auditorium. Here Mass would be celebrated for the next thirty-eight years. The school was highly successful; additions were built in 1957 and 1962. The school was run by the Felician Sisters, a work they would continue until 1988. At one time, during the period of the Baby Boom and when Catholic school students were permitted to ride public school buses, the school had as many as 575 students.

Because the Air Force Base had been the principal reason for the parish's existence, St. Philip Neri for many years knew a continuous turnover of military and civilian personnel. Not until the 1980's did the community begin to gel sufficiently for a permanent church to become a real possibility. Under the leadership of Father John Feehily, a church was built in 1992; it was dedicated by Archbishop Salatka on November 13 of that year. Nearly a thousand Catholic households are now on the parish register, with about 300 students in the school.

MUSTANG
Holy Spirit

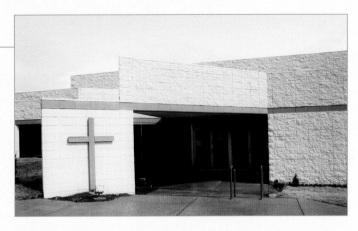

MUSTANG, midway between Yukon and Tuttle in eastern Canadian County, is roughly fourteen miles southwest of Oklahoma City. Father Larry Gatlin was appointed as first pastor of Holy Spirit parish on June 15, 1983; he would guide the parish through its first twelve years of life. The town itself, a relative newcomer named for a nearby creek, had few theatres or auditoriums, so the first Masses were offered in the chapel of a local funeral home. As religious education classes were organized, they were offered in daycare centers, bank meeting areas, and even the Methodist church. By March 1985 the parish had outgrown the funeral home and had moved to temporary quarters at the Town and Country Shopping Center.

The parish center and temporary church, at 1100 North Sara Road, were ready for occupancy by November 1985. In 1988 the second phase of development saw construction of a rectory and parish office. At present there are 320 families at Holy Spirit, and further growth is anticipated as the town continues to develop.

NICOMA PARK
Our Lady of Fatima

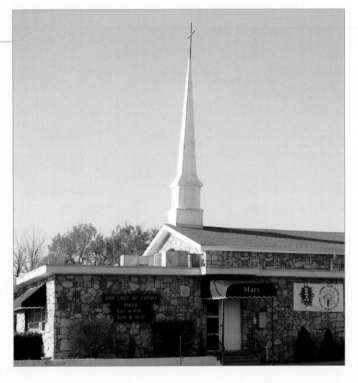

G.A. NICHOLS was the developer of this town east of Oklahoma City; his surname, combined with the word Oklahoma, gave the place its name. The Nicoma Park post office was established in 1929. For years the community was known as a center for chicken and egg production, but then a virus destroyed the baby chicks and the whole operation collapsed.

Monsignor John Walde, pastor of Corpus Christi parish, began organizing a parish in Nicoma Park in 1948. This led to Mr. and Mrs. H.V. Meyers making a donation of a house at Northeast 23rd and Meyers Circle. On November 1, 1949, Bishop McGuinness dedicated the main room of this house as Our Lady of Fatima chapel. The congregation consisted of about twenty families, and priests from Jones and Luther provided the parish staff. Additional property, including part of the chicken-raising operation, was purchased until the total amounted to three and a half acres. Here a new church was built in 1952, and priests from Corpus Christi offered Mass each Sunday.

Father Stephen MacAulay was appointed first resident pastor of Nicoma Park in 1957. His first order of business was to build a school. With three classrooms and a multi-purpose parish hall, the school opened in 1961 with 82 students in first through eighth grades. Dominican Sisters from Great Bend, Kansas, and a lay teacher provided the faculty. The school continued to serve the parish until 1984, when the usual combination of rising costs and declining income caused it to close.

In 1973 Our Lady of Fatima was the first parish in the Oklahoma City metropolitan area to join the Meals on Wheels program. After more than 30 years parish members still gather to serve a hot meal to about 35 shut-ins every Monday. In 1989 the parish undertook a complete renovation of the church, school, parish hall, and rectory. Archbishop Salatka rededicated the church on May 14, 1990.

NORMAN
St. Joseph

SEVERAL hundred people claimed lots on the Norman townsite the day of the Land Run, and the first Mass was offered there within two months. The first church went up in March 1890, but it was the beginning of 1896 before Norman achieved the status of a parish. In part this was because Purcell in the Chickasaw Nation was not far away. Purcell had, not only an established parish, but also St. Elizabeth's Mission School for Chickasaw Girls. The two towns were only ten miles apart and connected by the Santa Fe railroad, which meant that the pastor of Purcell could, with relative ease, look after the concerns of parishioners in Norman.

The first pastor was six-feet-four-inches tall, 24 years old, and two years ordained. His name was John Metter, and he would be the pastor at Norman until his death in 1923. He was from Colmar, in Alsace, a province that lies on the French-German border and that was fought over three times between 1870 and 1945. He had been a refugee in Algeria, and he was the third priest Bishop Meerschaert ordained.

Possessed of a fiery temper, but with energy to match, he immediately set about planning a larger church and a rectory. The church, dedicated on March 20, 1898, was dedicated to St. Joseph and St. Patrick. There had been some debate about the name, with one benefactor insisting the name be that of the Irish saint, while the parishioners preferred St. Joseph. Nationalities among the parish members may also have played a part, with an Irish contingent pitted against another of Germans.

Father Metter also had charge of a parish at Harrah, with instructions to offer Mass at McLoud, at Denver (some six miles east of Norman), and at "places on the Santa Fe line between Purcell and Ardmore." He opened an elementary school in 1898, staffed by Benedictine Sisters from St. Joseph's Convent in Guthrie. A high school would follow in 1909. Also in 1898 he had temporary charge of the parish at Edmond, where he built a church as well. Clearly impressed with this effort and success, Bishop Meerschaert recommended the priest for a papal honor. In 1900 Father Metter was named a monsignor, the first one in Oklahoma. He was not yet 30 years of age.

His later career, however, was not so promising. The Benedictine Sisters withdrew from the schools in 1914 because of problems in dealing with the pastor. In 1917 Monsignor Metter precipitated the famous Sacramental Wine Case (page 21), when he went to the Santa Fe station to pick up a case of altar wine he had ordered. Oklahoma had just passed the Bone Dry Law, which forbade the importation of alcoholic spirits. The case went all the way to the Oklahoma Supreme Court and attracted a great deal of attention, for the whole nation was debating the Prohibition issue at the time.

Once Metter had died, the parish could at last give its attention to something that would ordinarily have been part of its mission from the beginning. This was the situation of the Catholic students at the University of Oklahoma, which had existed in Norman since 1890. European-born priests viewed American public schools with suspicion, because European universities of the 19th century were hotbeds of anticlerical and irreligious agitation. Bishop Kelley, Meerschaert's successor, was not of this mindset, however, and he set about creating a Catholic student center at Norman. The priests in charge of this were at first from the Viatorian order, and for a time they also functioned as pastors at St. Joseph's.

Another concern of the Norman pastor would be the South Navy base constructed at Norman during World War II, and he was responsible for chaplaincy at Griffin Memorial Hospital, the state's major facility for the mentally ill. In 1949 the old church was pulled down and replaced with the present brick building in Colonial style. Bishop McGuinness formally opened this on February 15, 1951.

A major crisis occurred in the 1960's. The parish found itself with a school that was overcrowded, on one hand, while at the same time unable to subsidize it at the traditional, but unrealistically low, rate of tuition.

Parishioners were divided as to whether to construct larger facilities or downscale in favor of emerging religious education programs. The result was a new structure that attempted to meet both sets of expectations. It was no sooner up, though, than the Sisters of Divine Providence announced they could no longer staff the institution.

Parishes all across the nation faced similar problems, of course, and had to deal with the emotional and financial fallout. In recent years St. Joseph's has generated two additional parishes in Norman. Currently, it is providing service to the recent influx of Hispanic Catholics in the Norman area.

NORMAN

St. Mark the Evangelist

As early as 1961, Bishop Reed sought to obtain property on the west side of Norman for a parish, but nothing came of the idea then. Thirty years later, in 1991, Father John Metzinger was appointed pastor of what was at first called the Catholic Community of West Norman, The first Mass was offered on July 14, in the ballroom of the Sheraton Hotel, with more than 350 persons in attendance.

Ten acres had been purchased earlier on Tecumseh Road. In August a home was purchased adjacent to this property, to serve as a rectory and a planning center for the new buildings. It was the parish's goal to be in its new facility by Easter 1993, and on April 7, 1993, the Wednesday of Holy Week, Archbishop Beltran blessed the new parish center.

The parish began with 200 families. By the fall of 1997 there were 675 families, and plans were underway for the permanent church. The groundbreaking took place in 1998, and the large church, with seating for one thousand, was dedicated on December 6, 2000. The building is notable for its splendid narthex, or gathering area, and for its large marble baptistery.

A special concern of Archbishop Beltran has been preserving and expanding Catholic education through central and western Oklahoma. Thus in 1996, All Saints Catholic School was founded by the archdiocese itself to serve the community of Norman and surrounding area. It is supported by the three Norman parishes—St. Joseph's, St. Mark's and St. Thomas More—making it the only regional, or interparish, elementary school in the Archdiocese. The school campus is located about one-half mile from St. Mark's. Its dedication and official opening was held on November 8, 1998.

Father Metzinger had previously been an associate pastor of St. Thomas More, where he served with Father Thomas Boyer, pastor there from 1981 to 1987. In 2002, Father Boyer succeeded Father Metzinger at St. Mark's.

Norman
St. Thomas More

THE University of Oklahoma began life at Norman in 1892, but it developed slowly, and no thought was given to a Catholic ministry for the young men attending the school until the early years of the twentieth century. The impetus for this, such as it was, came from the lay members of the parish, because the longtime pastor at Norman opposed secular education on principle and wanted nothing to do with the university.

Only after his death in 1923, and the arrival of Bishop Kelley the next year, was any serious effort made to provide Catholic chaplaincy for the OU students. The students themselves formed a Newman Club in 1920; their first official act was to petition the bishop for a separate university parish. As late as 1961, though, the pastor of St. Joseph's in Norman was strenuously opposing any formal division of his parish.

In 1921 the Norman council of the Knights of Columbus built a house, costing $12,000, at 535 University Boulevard. It is not entirely clear what the purpose of this house was to be, but it became a dormitory for male Catholic students and was known as Columbia Hall. Title to the property passed to Bishop Kelley in 1925. At the same time the Bishop contracted with the Sisters of Divine Providence to build Newman Hall for Catholic female students. This three-story facility opened at the corner of Boyd and Chatauqua in February 1926.

Work then began on a chapel next door to Newman Hall. The bishop obtained a grant from Catholic Extension to pay for the chapel. One of Extension's donors was a Chicago woman who had attached to her donation the condition that a church built with her funds be named for a title in the Litany of the Blessed Virgin, Mother Most Admirable —in Latin, *Mater Admirabilis*. (The graceful little chapel with the unwieldy name still stands; it was sold in 1978 and is now a private residence, resulting from an innovative conversion that was featured on the Home and Garden Channel.)

The Viatorian Fathers from Chicago took charge of the chapel for a few years, then a friend of Bishop Kelley's from Detroit, Father Joseph Hallissey, served as chaplain until his death in 1951. In 1959 Father Ernest Flusche was appointed chaplain. He immediately requested a change of the chapel's name, which was approved the next year. Henceforth, the Catholic ministry at OU would be under the patronage of St. Thomas More.

The original Catholic student complex had been located close to the student housing of that period. By the early 1960's, however, the university was moving these facilities to the south and west. At the same time a new Catholic parish was being planned for the Oklahoma State University campus at Stillwater, and so it followed that a similar plan be enacted at Norman. In 1966 the process began when St. Thomas More was canonically erected as a parish independent of St. Joseph's.

Once again, however, the project stalled. A combination of factors was at fault, but they came down to the unsettled condition of society and the Church at the time. Money and personnel were at a premium, all the more so since it was obvious that the diocese would have to subsidize the entire project. The students could not be expected to carry the financial burden.

In 1973 the diocese was divided. The commitment to campus ministry shaped the diocesan boundary; the new Archdiocese of Oklahoma City would continue to be responsible for the Norman students, while the Diocese of Tulsa would take over the Stillwater ministry, along with its sizable debt and operating expense. On paper, the Tulsa diocese has a gerrymandered appearance, as its boundary swings out from the eastern third of the state to include Payne County.

Father William Ross arranged for the purchase of property on Stinson Street between Lincoln and Jenkins, but in 1976 the university parish was entrusted to the Friars of the Atonement, and in 1977 the parish contracted with Raymond Yeh, a member of the university faculty, to design a new Catholic student center. Father Michael Graham, S.A., was pastor during the construction period, which culminated on September 23, 1979, when Archbishop Charles Salatka dedicated the new facilities.

At the time the new building was completed, it was estimated that there were 2000 Catholic students at the university, along with some fifty faculty members and their families. In 1981 the St. Thomas More pastorate returned to the care of the diocesan clergy. Today, there are 6000 Catholic students and over 200 Catholic faculty members.

OKLAHOMA CITY
St. Andrew Dung-Lac

CATHOLIC communities on the East Coast of the U.S. are used to so-called national parishes, organized not by geography but by ethnicity. They became a feature of Catholic urban life beginning with the migration of large groups from Europe in the 1840's through the 1920's. Bishops in these places not infrequently have been bedeviled by various language groups demanding services in their own language. In recent years national parishes have again become an issue, as Hispanic and Oriental Catholics have increasingly migrated to this country, and to Oklahoma from other parts of the nation. Oklahoma bishops have been slow to create parishes for specific language groups, but the sheer preponderance here of Catholics whose first language is other than English has made it imperative to provide for their religious needs in their own language.

Thus it has happened that in 1994, almost twenty years after the first large migration following the end of the Vietnam War, the parish of St. Andrew Dung-Lac was established for Vietnamese Catholics in Oklahoma City. Andrew Dung Lac (1785-1839) was a Vietnamese martyr, canonized in 1988. St. Andrew's parish began at the Vietnamese Center at 2337 Northwest 19th Street, but in 1998 it relocated at Southwest 55th and South May Avenue. Today it provides an important and needed service to the Vietnamese community.

OKLAHOMA CITY
Korean Martyrs

FOR some years a Korean priest came from New York to offer Mass at the invitation of Korean Catholics in Oklahoma. In 1993 Father Jong Ki Kim, who was studying here, began saying Mass for the Koreans at St. Andrew Church in Moore, then at St. Paul Church in Del City. In October 1998 property was purchased and a parish located at 2600 Southwest 74th Street in Oklahoma City. The church was dedicated on December 20, 1998. The parish is staffed by a religious order, the Clerical Society of the Most Holy Trinity of Mirinae, from Korea.

OKLAHOMA CITY
Byzantine Mission

FURTHER displaying the endless variety and complexity of the Catholic Church worldwide is a small group of Oklahoma City Catholics whose ethnic heritage includes Eucharistic celebration according to the ancient Byzantine Rite. Besides the "Roman" or "Western" Catholic Church, there are 21 other ancient Catholic Churches that are in union with the pope, the Bishop of Rome. They are regarded as equal in dignity with the Roman Church, and they have their own bishops, called eparchs.

The Byzantine Catholic community of Oklahoma City is part of the Byzantine Catholic Metropolitan Church of Pittsburgh. His Eminence, Metropolitan Basil of Pittsburgh is the head and eparch of this Church. There are also three other dioceses of this Church in the United States whose members number 300,000 souls. Father Philip Seeton, who is authorized to offer the Eucharist in either the Latin or Byzantine Rite, leads this group, which meets regularly at the chapel of Bishop McGuinness High School.

OKLAHOMA CITY
Latin Mass Community

measures to guarantee respect for their rightful aspirations. In this matter I ask for the support of the bishops and of all those engaged in the pastoral ministry in the Church.

In the archdiocese a group of traditionally minded persons had taken the bold step of having a Latin Mass offered regularly at St. Michael Chapel in Bethany, a privately owned facility, without the approval of the archbishop. Father Jerome Talloen also offered a Latin Mass at the Catholic Pastoral Center chapel for years until his health failed. In 1995 Archbishop Beltran invited members of the Priestly Fraternity of St. Peter stationed in Tulsa to commute to Oklahoma City and minister to these Catholics with his blessing. Finally, in September of 2000 a full time resident priest of the Fraternity was assigned to Oklahoma City.

POPE JOHN PAUL II issued an apostolic letter on July 2, 1988 entitled *Ecclesia Dei* which read in part:

To all those Catholic faithful who feel attached to some previous liturgical and disciplinary forms of the Latin tradition, I wish to manifest my will to facilitate their ecclesial communion by means of the necessary

OKLAHOMA CITY
Corpus Christi

BISHOP Meerschaert died in February 1924, and his successor arrived in October. Before the month was out he had invited members of a small religious community from Duluth, Minnesota, to begin a Catholic census in Oklahoma City. This community was popularly known as the Pink Sisters, from the color of its habit, but its formal name was the Corpus Christi Sisters.

The results of the census showed that a new parish was needed on the east side of Oklahoma City, so in 1925 the bishop purchased ten lots at Eighth and Durland, the former residence of Oklahoma pioneer C.G. Jones. In August he appointed Father Peter Wilwerding as first pastor of Corpus Christi parish. Unfortunately this otherwise good priest was not up to the task of establishing so large a project. After a year he had built a combination church-school building, but the parish had a debt of $66,000, and no way to pay it.

The bishop next appointed Father John Walde as pastor, and things began to move at a good pace. Although it took ten years because of the Depression, the parish paid off its huge debt. In the meantime it had become obvious that the Jones property did not allow for future expansion, so in 1936 the bishop proposed that Catholic Charities take over the property. A square block at Fifteenth and Stonewall, called Kelley Park (no relation to the bishop), was available, and this became the new site of the parish. A new school building was built in 1937, and work began on a new church in 1944. Bishop McGuinness dedicated the splendid building in Spanish Colonial style on October 18, 1945. Two years later work began on a new convent for the sisters staffing the school; and in 1952, Father Walde, by now a monsignor, moved into a new rectory. The parish also sponsored a new mission church at Nicoma Park, Our Lady of Fatima, in 1948.

In 1922 the diocesan vicar for missions, Father Renier Sevens, had organized African American Catholics on the east side of Oklahoma City into what became St. Peter Claver parish. Mass was offered for a few years in a hall at Northeast Second and Stiles. In that frenetic year of 1925, Bishop Kelley invited an Irish order, the Holy Ghost Fathers, to take charge of the community. Property was purchased on Laird Avenue between Northeast Third and Fourth and a small church was built, but this proved undesirable and so St. Peter Claver moved to the 1100 block of Northeast Seventh and there built a church-school combination building that was dedicated on November 3, 1940. For over forty years the Holy Ghost Fathers operated a very active apostolate in the African-American community of Oklahoma City, but in 1967, facing reduced numbers, they were forced to withdraw from Oklahoma.

At the same time, Corpus Christi parish was experiencing growth of the black population on the east side, along with concomitant white flight. Bishop Reed, advised that it was time for a dramatic move that would help integrate the volatile neighborhood, decided to close St. Peter Claver and combine its membership with that of Corpus Christi. In the mistaken assumption that black Catholics would welcome the loss of their little parish, he neglected to consult them, and thus was forced to watch many of them angrily depart from the Church.

Into this very unfortunate situation now stepped the patient Father Herman Foken, who began slowly to rebuild what had been disrupted and destroyed. He was followed by a succession of priests who, each in his own way and with the help of many faithful parish members of both races, contributed toward the healing.

OKLAHOMA CITY
Christure the King

church was necessary, but a school was essential. Not only did a school offer their children a good basic education, but it helped promote Catholic values and a Catholic mindset at a time when most Catholics believed, not without reason, that their faith was under attack from the combined forces of the modern world.

The first parish building consisted of four classrooms and a chapel that seated 150. The median age of the adult parishioners was reflected in the fact that these classrooms were used for kindergarten and grades one through four. The first unit of a convent for the Benedictine Sisters was begun at the same time. There were two sisters, and in the 1949-50 school year they had seventy-two students under instruction. In 1951 four more classrooms were added, together with an expanded chapel. By 1960, as young couples continued to move into the increasingly upscale area, the school would have almost 500 students in eight grades.

Change in the Church is usually dated from the Second Vatican Council of 1962-65. In fact, many new Catholic movements were already at work in the U.S. The intellectual underpinnings of liturgical reform had begun in Europe in the 19th century, and the movement in this country can be dated from 1926. At Christ the King parishioners were encouraged to sing hymns at Mass and make the proper Latin responses to the prayers. The parish also had a parish council at an early date.

In 1959 Christ the King's pastor was named Bishop of Pueblo, Colorado. Bishop Buswell would serve twenty years in that post. At this writing he is still alive and well in retirement. His successor at Christ the King was Father Charles Conley, who had built a church in Norman and who would now oversee construction of the new church for Christ the King. Bishop Victor Reed dedicated it on September 16, 1962. Three bells in the 95-foot tower were named for bishops of Oklahoma, Francis (Kelley), Eugene (McGuinness), and Victor (Reed).

I N 1942 Bishop Kelley, by now in his seventies, entered into a prolonged and ultimately fatal illness. He did not die until 1948, but long before that arrangements were made to provide a healthy bishop for Oklahoma. Bishop Eugene McGuinness was appointed coadjutor–administrator with right of succession–in late 1944 and took office in January 1945.

World War II ended in August of that year, and the restrictions imposed by the conflict began to ease in the months that followed. Soldiers returned home, and an act of Congress, the so-called G.I. Bill of Rights, enabled them to finish their college educations even as they married, started families, and purchased new homes in the outlying areas of Oklahoma City.

By 1947 the new bishop was deep in plans to expand the diocese, and that year he decided that Our Lady of Perpetual Help parish should be divided, and a new parish established north of Northwest 50th Street. As pastor he appointed Father Charles Buswell, a curate at Our Lady's who also served as the bishop's master of ceremonies.

The diocese bought property at Elmhurst Avenue and Dorset Drive for $15,000, and the bishop conducted a groundbreaking ceremony in the spring of 1949. The parish began with 125 families. It may be difficult for modern Catholics to imagine, but the first priority of Catholics in establishing a parish in those days was not a place of worship, but a parochial school. They saw that a

Father Ernest Flusche was pastor of Christ the King from 1969 to 1978; by now the parish was recognized as the premier Catholic congregation in Oklahoma City. Its choir was outstanding, it was operating strong ministries to the community, and it was developing a healthy financial footing. The next pastor was Father Clement Pribil, just returned to Oklahoma from several years as rector of the American seminary attached to the University of Louvain. He was responsible for the new family center, with its gymnasium, meeting spaces, and parish offices. His time at Christ the King was comparatively short, caused by his death from cancer in 1984 at a young age. The family center was named in his honor. He was followed by Father Gerald Mayfield, who would serve twelve years and die in his next assignment at age 55. Father Joseph Ross has been pastor since 1995. During his tenure an ambitious three-phase "Step Into The Future" project was completed. It included major remodeling of the present school which included turning some of those rooms into parish offices, renovating the rectory and adding a large, functional gathering space (atrium-style) between the church and the new junior high wing. The final phase was completed September 30, 2001, with a ribbon-cutting ceremony and a Mass offered by Archbishop Beltran. The members of the parish have every right to be proud of their modern and spacious facilities.

OKLAHOMA CITY
Holy Angels

HOLY ANGELS parish, on the near northwest side of Oklahoma City, was divided from St. Joseph's in October 1926. Bishop Francis Kelley, then beginning his long episcopate in Oklahoma, believed that every priest with an appointment to diocesan-wide responsibilities should also have charge of a congregation. He had just appointed Father James A. Garvey to be the first director of Catholic Charities, and he asked him to move to a house on property that the diocese owned at Third and Blackwelder. Father Garvey was to organize a small parish on what then was almost the outskirts of the city.

The first Mass was in an old frame building that had been a barn and was later transformed into a community hall. A brick building, to serve at first as a church and then a school, was begun in March 1927. When the parish was started there were about 45 Catholic families, many of them elderly and poor, living within its limits.

Father James Garvey's nephew, Father John Garvey, was ordained in 1933, and the next year he became assistant to his uncle at both Catholic Charities and at Holy Angels. In 1940 he succeeded to the parish as pastor.

In 1949 Father James Garvey, by now a monsignor, died, and was succeeded by Father A.A. Isenbart. Later, when the younger Father Garvey retired, Father Isenbart also became pastor. Father Isenbart built the present Holy Angels Church in 1950, but his responsibilities at Catholic Charities had by then grown to the point that he could not administer these and the parish as well.

In the 1960's the neighborhood around Holy Angels began to change for the worse. By this time Father John Walch, noted Oklahoma artist, was living in the former convent. The school had recently closed, and he established the St. John Damascene School of Liturgical Art there. Father Walch served as pastor at Holy Angels until his retirement in 1989.

Archbishop Charles Salatka had come to see the need for an additional parish to serve the need of Hispanics in Oklahoma City. Father Donald Wolf was appointed pastor, and Deacon Lucio Nieto began working full time for the parish. The Missionary Carmelite Sisters of St. Teresa came from Mexico to establish a convent in the parish. They have been in residence at Holy Angels Parish for twenty years. In spite of recurrent vandalism endemic to the neighborhood, the parish has continued to grow. The church was fully renovated and consecrated in 1997. There are now 250 families, of whom 218 are from Mexico, Guatemala, Nicaragua, Honduras, Argentina, and Colombia.

Church of the Epiphany of the Lord

OKLAHOMA CITY
Epiphany of the Lord

within the territory, parishioners logically gravitated to the center's chapel during Epiphany's first years.

Father Philip Bryce was the founding pastor. Within its first twenty years, the parish grew tenfold to 1200 families. Even as it developed numerically, so it did spiritually, with new programs and ministries, and physically, with a progressive schedule of construction on property that was originally part of the St. Francis de Sales Seminary (later the Center for Christian Renewal and now the Catholic Pastoral Center).

The first unit (now Bryce Hall) was dedicated in 1980, a rectory in 1982, the permanent church in 1984, and a family center in 1997. Epiphany underwent great sorrow as well, as the Murrah Building bombing robbed it of two fine young parishioners, Julie Welch and Mark Bolte. Their stories are included in Maria Scaperlanda's book, *Their Faith Touched Us: The Legacy of Three Young Oklahoma City Bombing Victims.* Epiphany parish now has a membership of over 1500 families.

E PIPHANY parish began with 120 families on June 16, 1976, when Archbishop John R. Quinn formally established the parish north of Wilshire Boulevard and west of Meridian. Because the Catholic Pastoral Center (then known as the Center for Christian Renewal) lay

OKLAHOMA CITY
Immaculate Conception

A LTHOUGH it began in its present form in the 1950's, Immaculate Conception parish actually dates to 1890, when a group of German farmers settled southwest of Oklahoma City. They had come from Nodaway County, in far northwest Missouri, where Swiss Benedictine monks had founded Conception Abbey in 1873. The farmers named their settlement Conception. In 1892 a small church dedicated to the Immaculate Conception was built as a mission of St. Joseph's (and later of Sacred Heart); it was located near the present intersection of Meridian and Southwest 44th Street. Classes were held in the church until 1902, when a separate church building was constructed. The parish continued, though with a dwindling congregation, until it was finally closed in 1930.

During the Catholic renaissance that followed World War II, Bishop McGuinness reconstituted the congregation as a mission (again) of Sacred Heart parish. Original plans were to rebuild at the former location, but the airport authority objected, in view of its own plans for

expansion, so a new site was chosen at 3901 Southwest 29th Street. Ground was broken in 1952 for a chapel, school, and convent. Two years later Immaculate Conception became an independent parish for the first time, with Father A.O. Murphy as pastor. The school continued until 1968, with Sisters of Mercy, Extension Lay Volunteers, and other lay teachers on the staff. Influenced by the Second Vatican Council, the parish renovated the church interior in 1986 and added air conditioning. Immaculate Conception observed its centennial in 1992, and in 1998 it dedicated a prayer garden to the victims of the Murrah bombing.

In 1942 the original church was sold to a Methodist congregation at Wheatland. Moved to the neighborhood of Council Road and Southwest 79th Street, the small frame building still stands, more than a century after its construction.

OKLAHOMA CITY
Little Flower (Our Lady of Mount Carmel)

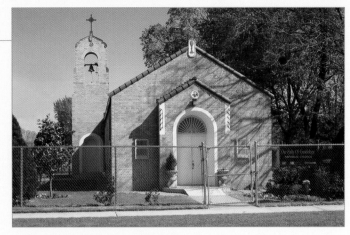

✧ Our Lady of Guadalupe Church.

I N 1910 the Mexican Revolution resulted in a persecution of the Catholic Church, which continued for many years. In 1914 three Spanish priests of the Discalced (barefoot) branch of the Carmelite Order arrived in Oklahoma from their mission in Torreon, where they had escaped the army of Pancho Villa. They began a ministry in the coalfields around Hartshorne, but in 1921 several of them relocated to Oklahoma City, where a Hispanic population had begun to develop on the south side.

In 1926 Bishop Kelley authorized the Carmelites to begin construction of the present large brick church at 1100 South Walker Boulevard. The church of Our Lady of Mount Carmel was dedicated in March 1927. A year later, the newly completed main altar was installed and dedicated to St. Therese of Lisieux, a young Carmelite nun who had died in 1897, was canonized in 1925, and was known as the Little Flower of Jesus.

The Sisters of the Third Order of Mount Carmel and St. Therese, a community organized by Father Edward Soler, O.C.D., at Bentley, Oklahoma, in 1917, established a convent on the grounds of the Oklahoma City parish and began a school for Spanish-speaking children. The Carmelite Fathers opened a second church in Oklahoma City in 1937, Our Lady of Guadalupe, in the Packing Town area.

Little Flower parish and school have served the

Catholic Hispanic community of Oklahoma City for over 75 years, assisting thousands of immigrants from Mexico and South Texas to integrate fully into the larger Anglo society. Father Louis Scagnelli, O.C.D., pastor of Little Flower for many years, was the first vicar for Hispanics in the archdiocese. He spent much energy visiting the different Hispanic communities, encouraging them and keeping in touch through a radio program. He also brought to Oklahoma City the Eucharistic Missionary Sisters of St. Teresa from Mexico to work with Spanish-speaking people in Oklahoma City.

Father Jesus Sancho, O.C.D., continued the work of Father Louis and worked hard to make the U.S. Immigration and Naturalization Service's amnesty program a success at Little Flower. Thousands of families regularized their immigration situation with the help of a very large team of parishioners formed to help them. Classes in English are a regular part of the parish's ministry to its newcomers. In 1990 the Little Flower clinic was opened in cooperation with St. Anthony Hospital. It is the only Oklahoma City clinic with a staff that speaks both Spanish and English.

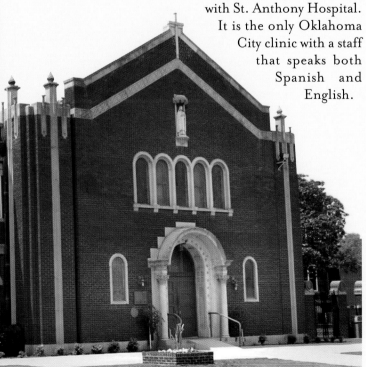

✧ Little Flower Church.

OKLAHOMA CITY
Our Lady of Perpetual Help Cathedral

T HE third parish in Oklahoma City was founded by decree of Bishop Meerschaert on January 16, 1919. Father Albert Monnot, then pastor of Hinton, was named to organize the parish that would cover 80 square miles to serve the northwest expansion of the city.

The origin of the parish's name is uncertain, but Bishop Meerschaert had great devotion to Mary under a similar title, Our Lady of Prompt Succor. The Ursuline Sisters in New Orleans maintained a shrine in her honor, and the bishop believed he had been saved from almost certain death from kidney disease some years before by the prayers said for him there.

The first Masses were celebrated in an automobile showroom on Classen Boulevard. In May a dozen men worked for two days to put up a temporary wooden church building, 30 by 60 feet, on land recently acquired by the parish—the same property, at Northwest 32nd Street and Lake Avenue, that the parish occupies today. In June ground was broken for a permanent church-school building, and in September the school opened with classes taught by three Sisters of Mercy. The school offered twelve grades, and 90 children enrolled the first year. Within two years there were 180 students and seven faculty members.

Construction began on the new church in July 1923. The pastor's brother, a successful architect, designed the building. In February 1924 the last brick was laid, but that month Bishop Meerschaert died. His successor, Bishop Kelley, did not arrive in Oklahoma until the fall, and he was installed at St. Joseph's Cathedral by Cardinal George Mundelein of Chicago on October 15. The next day the cardinal presided at the dedication of Our Lady's Church, and the new bishop offered there his first pontifical Mass in Oklahoma.

On November 14, 1930, the see that had been called the Diocese of Oklahoma since its creation in 1905 became officially the Diocese of Oklahoma City and Tulsa. The church of Our Lady of Perpetual Help became a cathedral, along with Holy Family Church in Tulsa. In 1932 the parish school was renamed as well; thereafter it was known as

John Carroll School in honor of the first Catholic bishop of the United States.

In 1947 the cathedral underwent the first of several extensive renovations. On October 15 of that year Bishop McGuinness presided at a solemn consecration of the church. In 1950 a new diocesan high school, eventually to be named for Bishop McGuinness, opened, and from that point John Carroll functioned solely as an elementary school.

In 1973 the Diocese of Oklahoma City and Tulsa was divided, and the central and western part of the state became the Archdiocese of Oklahoma City, with its cathedral at Our Lady's. In 1975 a further church renovation resulted in a new Eucharistic chapel in the base of the bell tower. The baldachin formerly over the main altar was moved to this chapel to adorn the shrine of the Blessed Sacrament.

Vietnamese refugees began to arrive in Oklahoma City in July 1975; 30 families made their home in the cathedral parish, and a Vietnamese priest, Father Can Dinh, was appointed to care for them. As more Vietnamese arrived, the ministry was expanded and Father Anthony Bao was named associate pastor in 1980.

The next major renovation was carried out in 1993. Known as *Renaissance*, this involved a new roof on the church, a new baptistery, and a new lighting system. As work continued, a new garage, a new classroom building and gymnasium, and underground utilities were added. In 1995 the cathedral received a new Zimmer pipe organ. The Connor Center, originally built in 1975, was completely redesigned in 2000, with the addition of Renaissance Plaza and the Chapel of All Saints.

Oklahoma City
Sacred Heart

BECAUSE Oklahoma City is divided by the North Canadian River, it was inevitable that St. Joseph's parish, north of the river, would be matched by a second parish to its south. There was another factor. After the fire that destroyed Sacred Heart Abbey and St. Mary's Academy in 1901, the Sisters of Mercy relocated to Oklahoma City, where, on the highest elevation in town, they built Mount Saint Mary Academy.

This ambitious undertaking gradually attracted Catholics (and others) south of the river as well. In 1909 Bishop Meerschaert bought ten lots from the Sisters of Mercy, just across Shartel Avenue from the school itself. Then, on November 9, 1910, he appointed Father James F. McGuire as first pastor of the new parish, to be called Sacred Heart.

Nothing ever goes smoothly, of course, and a debate immediately developed between parishioners who wanted to settle the parish on the property obtained by the bishop, and others who preferred another location on Central Avenue. The group that favored the original site invited a number of men from the area who realized that a new church would be good for the neighborhood, and hence for business. These additional voters, many of them non-Catholic, ensured victory for the adherents of the Shartel Avenue site. After this colorful beginning, the first parish Mass was celebrated at "the Mount" on April 11, 1911.

The first church was constructed soon thereafter. Reflecting the blue-collar economic stratum of the parish, it was a simple wooden affair, measuring 70 by 30 feet, and completely bare of decoration inside. During the week it was divided into two classrooms by a heavy canvas curtain, which was raised on Friday afternoon and the space rearranged for Sunday Mass. Weekday Masses were offered at the chapel of Mount Saint Mary's. This multi-purpose structure served the parish for fully nine years, until it was moved aside and the new church constructed in its place.

Under the parish's second pastor, Father John T. Hall, Sacred Heart built a new brick rectory and then began work on a matching church. World War I had just ended, and there was a building boom going on in Oklahoma City. Construction materials and experienced workers were scarce. As a result, only the basement of the new church was finished by the fall of 1920.

The basement was used as the first church had been, for school during the week and for Mass on Sunday. But it leaked, and badly. During the spring rains of 1921, the schoolchildren were sometimes soaked up to their ankles.

The situation was saved when the bishop obtained a $35,000 loan, and the shell of the church was finished by Christmas 1921. Even though the interior was still unfinished, Bishop Meerschaert dedicated the new building on January 2, 1922. When entirely furnished, it cost $65,000.

Always strapped for cash, the parish continued to use the original church for classrooms, though by this time the building was in bad shape. Finally, in 1924, the parish obtained a new brick school. A man who owned a farm near the river gave it to the parish, which sold the land and used the proceeds, about $7,500.00, to build the eight-room school. This building served for another 20 years, until it too was pulled down and replaced by another, which was dedicated in 1946. At the time, the school's enrollment was 243. Ten years later, the school was equipped with a gymnasium at a cost of $170,000. Although the parish debt seemed enormous at the time, the building paid for itself through the heavy usage it received and the support it gave to building up the parish community.

Unlike many parishes that have had to give up their parochial schools, Sacred Heart, fortified with the presence nearby of the Sisters of Mercy, has managed to keep its school open to this day. Among the changes the parish has seen has been an increase in the number of Hispanic families, to the point where there are now two Masses in Spanish at Sacred Heart every weekend.

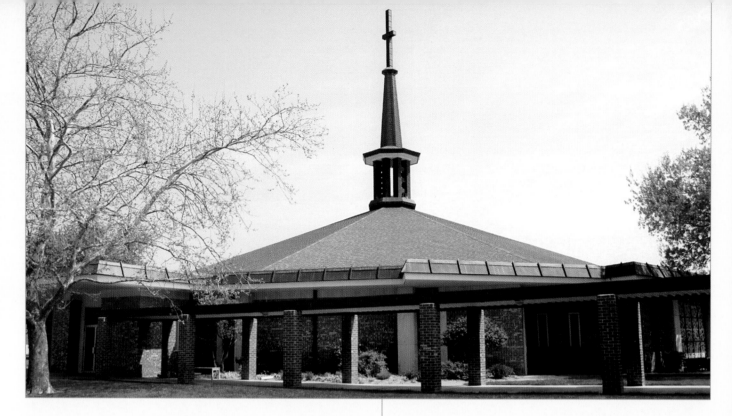

ON MAY 15, 1954, this parish began its existence in the Warr Acres suburb of Oklahoma City, with parishioners and territory drawn from the parishes of St. Patrick and Christ the King in Oklahoma City and St. John Nepomuk in Yukon. The founding pastor was Father Charles Beckman, whose baptismal patron became the titular of the parish.

At first the congregation of 55 families worshipped at the chapel of the cloistered Carmelite nuns, whose convent was then at Northwest 39th Street and Meridian Boulevard. On a site made possible through the generosity of Charles H. Makins, the parish constructed its first building, the present Beckman Hall. Father Beckman offered the first Mass on the parish property on Pentecost Sunday, May 29, 1955. The facility's west wing served as classrooms for 115 elementary students, and the three Carmelite Sisters of St. Therese lived in a convent built at the same time. They were replaced with Sisters of Charity of the Blessed Virgin Mary in 1956. In its first ten years, the parish grew to 635 families. The school enrollment stood at 408 students, and in 1964 there were 182 children in the religious education program for public school students.

Father John F. Lynch was the parish's second pastor from 1965 to 1968, and it was during his time in office that the permanent church was built, with its fine windows by the French master Gabriel Loire. The parish also developed in line with the currents of the Second Vatican Council; the Christian Family Movement had numerous cells at St. Charles, and the parish had a growing social consciousness as well.

Collaboration among the priests, sisters, and laity identified St. Charles's as a community "called by the Word to serve the world." Diverse and lively liturgies, comprehensive religious education, and committed social

OKLAHOMA CITY
St. Charles Borromeo

action were signs that the Spirit was fashioning a people of faith.

As St. Charles concluded its first 20 years, its membership stood at over a thousand families. Even as it had developed from the growth of longer-established communities, so did it engender in its turn a new parish. In 1976 part of the northwest corner of St. Charles was incorporated into the newly-formed Epiphany of the Lord parish. Such was the growth of the whole area, however, that within a year the parish roll at St. Charles was as large as it had been before.

In the 1980's the parish turned its attention to stewardship and to deepening its staffing base. It had already obtained fulltime directors of social ministry, youth and religious education; now it added a fulltime director of liturgy, and it moved in the direction of total family involvement in religious education.

In 1993 the St. Charles Clinic opened, to provide free health services and medical care to those who could not otherwise afford these; physicians, nurses, and support staff work on a volunteer basis. A new activity center integrated the existing structures for the school, the parish offices, and Beckman Hall with a new gymnasium, a nursery, youth room, and additional classrooms and meeting spaces. Archbishop Beltran dedicated this new facility on November 30, 1997. Six priests and four permanent deacons have arisen from the ranks of St. Charles parishioners.

OKLAHOMA CITY
St. Francis of Assisi

WHEN Bishop Kelley arrived in Oklahoma in 1924, he settled in the large home on the northwest side that had been built for his predecessor. Until recently this area had been mostly farmland, but it was rapidly filling up with urban development and city dwellers, a few of them Catholic. There was a small chapel in the bishop's residence, and these parishioners without a parish attended Mass there. By August 1925 their numbers had grown to the point that Bishop Kelley appointed a pastor for them. By 1927 this was Father John Van den Hende, and he built the first structure to serve the new parish, a small chapel attached to the residence at ground level. He also built a school.

With the onset of the Great Depression, Bishop Kelley, in order to save money, moved out of the residence and took rooms at St. Anthony Hospital. This meant that the residence could now serve as the rectory, school, and convent for St. Francis parish. In 1936 a larger brick chapel replaced the one built by Father Van den Hende. Sisters of Mercy staffed the school until 1938, when they were replaced by Dominican Sisters from Sinsinawa, Wisconsin. Because of the close association of the Dominicans with devotion to the Rosary, the school became known as Rosary School.

Father Everard Vander Grinten became pastor in 1933. In 1941, as the parish continued to grow, he announced plans for a new school. Because of wartime restrictions on building materials, the school could not be opened until three years later. As soon as the war ended, the parish began work on a new church. This was completed and dedicated on May 22, 1947. In the years since, the parish has been blessed with a succession of strong pastors who have made significant contributions to its buildings and programs. There currently are over 1000 families in the parish and 200 students in the school.

✦ The bishop's residence, which became the foundation for St. Francis of Assisi parish.

OKLAHOMA CITY
St. Joseph

A T Oklahoma Station, soon to be Oklahoma City, the first Catholic Mass was offered in J.K. McGinley's grocery-store tent on California Street on May 5, 1889, the second Sunday after the Run. The celebrant was Father N.F. Scallan, an itinerant priest from Iowa (see page 12), who had arrived just days before. At first located in Purcell, he soon moved to the future capital city, and plans got underway for a church. The first frame structure was put up on the slope of Blue Hill, just north of town, near the intersection of Fourth and Harvey. The pioneer church was 25 by 60 feet in size, with a steeple 63 feet high. The bell, which weighed 650 pounds, had been bought at the bargain price of $101.00. A small organ cost 40 dollars. The new church was dedicated in honor of St. Joseph on August 4. It served until the present church was built.

A new brick church, built across the street from the first one, opened on June 21, 1903. Two years later it was designated the cathedral of the new Diocese of Oklahoma. It served as Bishop Meerschaert's headquarters from then until his death in 1924. In 1930, however, the Holy See ordered that the see be restyled the Diocese of Oklahoma City and Tulsa. A north side church, Our Lady of Perpetual Help, was named cathedral, and St. Joseph's became known as the Old Cathedral.

During most of its existence, St. Joseph's sponsored a parochial school, which stood just across Harvey Avenue. When the school closed in 1966, the land it occupied was sold to the federal government, which built the Alfred P. Murrah Building there. On April 19, 1995, the Murrah

Building, and St. Joseph's next to it, made history when they were at the center of the great bomb blast that killed 168 men, women, and children, in what was, until then, the greatest act of terrorism ever committed on U.S. soil. St. Joseph's, though heavily damaged, was spared destruction because it was at the side of the building opposite where the blast occurred. Contributions from all over the world came in to repair the church, which reopened in a joyful ceremony in 1996.

✧ Interior of St. Joseph's after the Murrah Building bombing in 1995.

OKLAHOMA CITY
St. James

ST. JAMES' parish was established on Oklahoma City's south side in 1954, on seven acres of land which the diocese purchased from the Reding family. Monsignor Cecil E. Finn was the first pastor. Construction began promptly, the congregation took possession in July 1956, and the entire parish complex was dedicated as a unit on November 21 of that year.

Four years later, a large hall and a spacious new church were built. These additions were blessed by Bishop Reed in November 1960. In January 1971, however, the church was destroyed by fire. Once again, reconstruction began promptly and the new church was ready for its blessing in November.

Father Philip Donohoe, pastor from 1972 to 1980, was responsible for reducing the large debt which the parish had incurred over the years. Pentecost Sunday, 1979, was a special day because the congregation could burn its mortgage. In 1982, the parish built a family center and additional classrooms. An extensive renovation and construction project was completed during the pastorate of Father Robert T. Wood. The beautiful edifice was dedicated by Archbishop Beltran on November 6, 2001.

OKLAHOMA CITY ◈ St. Eugene

BISHOP Eugene J. McGuinness died suddenly on December 27, 1975. Six months later, his successor, Bishop Victor J. Reed, appointed Father James Ross as the first pastor of a new parish on the far north side of Oklahoma City, to be named in honor of Pope St. Eugene I (654-657), the baptismal patron of the late bishop.

Of the original 50 families, only five were older than fifty. According to Father Ross, the rest all had a great many small children, with more coming along each year. Of course, this was the pattern among suburban communities, especially Catholic ones, all over the country at the time.

At present the demographic spread at St. Eugene's is more balanced. Among its 1600 families today, there are more than 900 seniors, an equal number of young single adults, as well as the usual percentage of two-parent households. It is also an ethnically diverse parish, representing immigrants from 29 different countries.

Reflecting its rapid growth, St. Eugene's has had five stages of physical development. To the original church and school was added a larger church in 1965, a new community center in 1974, and an enlarged gymnasium in 1978. The present school was opened in 1997, and the parish is now awaiting a new church.

OKLAHOMA CITY
St. Patrick

out in a single day. With Father Donald Brooks, associate pastor, as the construction boss, parishioners cut the stone floor, built the altar screen, and made pews. Only the structural steel, concrete, and electrical work were hired out to others.

A special feature of the church is a series of gigantic angels, designed by the art consultant, Frank Kacmarcik, of Collegeville, Minnesota. Working from his design, the people built a wooden form, and then, once the concrete had been poured and a crane had lifted the 50 huge panels into place, the parishioners finished out the walls. After almost 500 people had worked for two years on the building, Bishop Reed blessed it on September 23, 1962. Since then, the remarkable structure has been honored with architectural awards no less than 28 times.

Although the wonderful church became the heart of the parish, its soul remained the school. When the financial and personnel crises of the 1960's caused the school to close in 1969, the trauma and division among the people of St. Patrick's was severe and lasting.

In the years that followed, however, the parish rallied. It became debt-free, built a new chapel for the Blessed Sacrament, beautified its grounds, and developed many ministries, especially to the sick and elderly.

JUST four days before St. Ann's Home, Catholic Charities' new facility for the aged, opened on the west side of Oklahoma City, the first Mass was said in its chapel for the members of a new parish. The date was June 10, 1950. Celebrant of the Mass was Father Michael McNamee, temporary chaplain of the home and founding pastor of St. Patrick's. Since he was a native of Ireland, it is not hard to see how the parish came by its titular.

St. Patrick's had 120 founding families. Ground was broken for the first parish building in January 1951. It contained an auditorium seating 325 and classrooms for eight grades. Masses began in the auditorium in August and the school opened the next month, staffed by the Sisters of Charity of Leavenworth, Kansas.

The second pastor was Monsignor Don J. Kanaly. He had studied in Europe and was much inspired by the vision of ordinary people working together to raise the great cathedrals of the Middle Ages. He believed that an American parish could literally build its own church. The people of St. Patrick's were themselves laborers, and the parish did not have much money. What they did have was their own talent and willingness to work, combined with the leadership of their pastor.

The effort began in 1959 with a test project, construction of a stone wall along Portland Avenue. Sixty men, working on six weekends and using 250 tons of rock, built a solid wall 50 feet long and six feet high. It still stands.

After the architect (Robert L. Jones, of Tulsa) and the engineer for the intricate, multifaceted roof (Enrique Candela, of Mexico City) had done their work, members of the parish began the excavation and foundation work. As many as a hundred workers turned

Union City
St. Joseph

THE first Mass in Union City, which first was called Sherman, was celebrated in Joseph Strunk's little hotel, by Father Joseph Beck of Hennessey, in early 1893. The next year Father A.G. Borremans, pastor of Okarche, supervised construction of the first church. On May 1, 1894, Bishop Meerschaert dedicated this in honor of his own baptismal patron, St. Theophile, or Theophilus. This was the only church in Oklahoma ever so dedicated. Stone for the church foundation was hauled on wagons across the North Canadian when the river ran dry enough to permit it.

St. Theophile's did not stand for long. A tornado demolished it in 1896, and the church that replaced it was named for St. Joseph. This was not opened, however, until 1899, apparently because the town was slow to recover from the tornado. In fact, the parish did not grow sufficiently to have a resident pastor until 1909, in the meantime being cared for as a mission variously from El Reno, Chickasha, and Anadarko.

Even before the parish received a pastor, however, it managed to build its own school. St. Joseph's school opened in 1907 with two Sisters of Divine Providence as its faculty. Father Peter Paul Schaeffer was the first resident pastor, and he purchased the large tract whereon is now located the parish complex. The third church was destroyed by fire in 1930, but its replacement was dedicated within the year.

Union City Catholics have traditionally been of German or Czech nationality, and they have given numerous vocations to the church in Oklahoma. These include Fathers John Demmer (ordained in 1914, died in the influenza pandemic of 1918), Daniel Fletcher, Wencelaus Michalicka, O.S.B., Florian Demmer O.S.B., and John Michalicka, together with over half a dozen Sisters in various communities.

The parish school closed in 1963. A huge tornado struck the parish buildings on May 24, 1973, flattening St. Joseph's school, convent, and parish hall, and heavily damaging the church. Repairs were made, and new stained glass windows were added to the church. In 1993 St. Joseph's, bloody but unbowed, observed a century of Catholic life in Union City.

❖ Msgr. Daniel Fletcher

❖ Father John Michalicka

YUKON
St. John Nepomuk

BEFORE there was Yukon, there was Frisco, a small settlement named for a proposed railroad that, when built, missed the town entirely. Frisco's post office was established in May 1889. Yukon came into existence nearly two years later, and in time Frisco was absorbed into Yukon. Local folklore says the town got its name because one of its founders saw the area as "a little gold mine."

Before there was a Czech Republic, there was the Kingdom of Bohemia, and many of the first settlers in Frisco-Yukon were Bohemians. Bohemia has long posed a special problem for Catholic missioners, because its history includes an early dispute with the priest John Hus, who had differences with the Church regarding matters of discipline and papal authority. Hus was executed as a heretic, and his angry followers eventually became the Moravian Brethren, who would have a profound influence on the development of Lutheranism a century after Hus. In its concern to keep Catholic Bohemians within the Church, American bishops have had to manage the further problem of the Bohemian language. In the Oklahoma

Territory this was akin to providing pastoral care to large numbers of Vietnamese in this country after the fall of Saigon, or to serving migrants who speak only Spanish. There were not many Bohemian-speaking priests in early Oklahoma, so providing for Bohemian farmers in Yukon, Union City, and Prague would always be difficult.

The parish of St. John Nepomuk, named for one of Bohemia's most popular saints, was begun in 1894, even though priests had been visiting Frisco and Yukon since the time of the Land Run. A small church was built that year, and Bishop Meerschaert dedicated it on November 7. Priests from Oklahoma City, Norman, and Hennessey cared for St. John's until 1906, when Father Joseph Lusar was named the first resident pastor. He had serious personality problems, however, and a later writer would credit him with the defection from the Faith of many of the Bohemian Catholics in Oklahoma.

After Father Lusar's departure the director of nearby St. Joseph's Orphanage took on additional duties as pastor of St. John's for several years. A larger church was built in 1902 on what became the corner of Eighth and Oak. This served for over half a century, until under Father Joseph Mazaika the third, and present, church was built in 1960-61. A Catholic school opened in Yukon in 1953. As this is written, it is still going strong.

The Oklahoma Panhandle

May 2, 1890

RECORDS of the famous expedition of Francisco Coronado into the American heartland (1540-1542) do not say with certainty if the expedition marched northward through what is now Oklahoma, or whether the trek was farther west, through the present Texas Panhandle. It is known, though, that Coronado and his fellow explorers did cross the Oklahoma Panhandle on their way back to Mexico.

The narrow appendage that gives Oklahoma its distinctive shape began life because of the famous Missouri Compromise of 1820. In that decision of the U.S. Congress, the principle was laid down that every state north of 36 degrees, 30 minutes of North Latitude (i.e., the Mason-Dixon Line) was to be a state where slavery would be forbidden —except for Missouri, which actually straddled the line— while every state south of the line would be a slave state.

Texas entered the Union in 1845, but its boundaries were not set until 1850. Because Texans wanted slaves, they could not extend their state boundary north of the Mason-Dixon Line. When the Kansas Territory was organized in 1854, it took the 37th Parallel as its south boundary, leaving an orphan strip about 200 miles long and half a degree of latitude wide (about 35 miles). This became known variously as No Man's Land, the Cimarron Territory, Beaver County (because of the North Canadian River, called the Beaver River in the Panhandle), and even the Land of Beaver. It tried to enter as an independent U.S. state, and at one point wanted to be an independent country. During the 1880's it had its own territorial representative in Congress. When the federal government finally got around to organizing the newly-opened territory of the Unassigned Lands, in May 1890, the Panhandle was legally attached to the Oklahoma Territory, even though the two were geographically separated by the Cheyenne-Arapaho Reservation. At statehood in 1907, three counties were created, each defined by the 100th through the 103rd Meridians of Longitude.

The first Catholic church in No Man's Land was built on the Lujan Ranch, practically at the very end of the Panhandle, in what is now Cimarron County. Juan Baca, a sheep rancher, had lured his wife from Colorado with the promise of her own chapel. Through the guidance of a Jesuit missionary from Trinidad, Colorado, Good Shepherd Chapel was built in 1893, and in 1894 Bishop Meerschaert, traveling by train and by horse and buggy, made a 1600-mile round trip through Kansas, Colorado, and New Mexico to dedicate it.

Guymon

May 2
1890

BOISE CITY
Good Shepherd

Wheeless, the Good Shepherd Chapel. In 1930 the chapel was still standing, though it had long been closed; a few ranch buildings are all that remain today.

In 1961 Bishop Reed established the parish of St. Philip Benizi, with Father John Scheller as pastor. Father Scheller took pride in the fact that, given the peculiar location of Boise City, he was actually nearer to six other diocesan bishops than to his own in Oklahoma City. An attractive church was built, which ultimately became attached to the parish in Guymon. In recent years the parish titular was changed from St. Philip to Good Shepherd, to honor the original Catholic foundation in Cimarron County.

CIMARRON County, of which Boise City is the seat, has had for years the distinction of being so sparsely settled that there is not one stoplight in the entire county. As noted above, the first Catholic church was on the Lujan ranch, near present-day

BEAVER
St. Frances Cabrini

BEFORE Bishop Francis Clement Kelley came to Oklahoma, he was founder and president of the Catholic Extension Society in Chicago. In December 1917 he was asked to preach at the funeral there of an Italian nun who had come to the U.S. in 1880 and become a naturalized citizen. She was Mother Frances Xavier Cabrini, foundress of the Sacred Heart Sisters with a special mission from Pope Leo XIII to care for the needs of Italian immigrants in the New World. Like Mother Teresa of Calcutta in later years, she was immensely active in developing her ministry in both North and South America. Two years before Bishop Kelley's death in 1948, he had the satisfaction of seeing Mother Cabrini named the first American citizen canonized saint.

The next year, 1947, saw the construction of a new Catholic church in the county seat of Beaver County. It was natural that it should receive the name of the new American saint. The first Mass was offered in the Beaver County Court House by Father Noel William, O.F.M.,

from Guymon. Later that year, lots in Beaver were donated and a former schoolhouse was purchased, moved to the property, and remodeled as a church.

A previous Beaver County church, St. Peter's, had been built on the Kollman brothers farm just north of the Texas state line. This was moved a mile or two south to Booker, Texas, where it still stands.

In 1963 care of Beaver was transferred from the Franciscans at Guymon to the pastor of Buffalo. In 1978 Beaver became one of the parishes served from Woodward.

HOOKER
Sacred Heart

story rectory; that year, too, St. Peter's in Guymon was begun as a mission of Hooker. In 1909, however, Guymon became the parish, with Hooker its mission, and matters have stood that way ever since.

At some point —it is not clear just when— the Hooker mission was closed. It reopened in 1944. Among the earliest parishioners at Hooker were John and Julia Schaapveld. Their son, Vernon, acted as custodian of the church; when he died in 1976, he left funds in his will for the construction of a new church. The new Sacred Heart was dedicated on May 25, 1980, on property several blocks from the original church. The old building was then converted to a parish outreach facility, operated by Hooker parish members until this day.

FATHER David Dunne became pastor of Amarillo, Texas, in 1904. He made trips into the Oklahoma Panhandle, especially to the area around Guymon, at least once a year until the time of his death in 1916.

Hooker first appears in the *Official Catholic Directory* of 1906 as being attended by Father Peter Kamp of Woodward. The first Sacred Heart Church was built that year. Hooker became a parish in 1907, with its own two-

GUYMON
St. Peter

IT appears that the Guymon mission received its name through the influence of Father Peter Kamp, pastor of Woodward, who assisted in the construction of its first church. The first St. Peter's was built in 1907. When Father Albert Monnot was appointed pastor of Hooker in 1909, he transferred the parish to Guymon, the county seat.

From 1916 until 1922, the pastor of Dalhart, Texas, cared for Guymon and its missions at Hooker and at the Kollman farm in Beaver County. Father Harold Pierce was pastor from 1935 to 1939; during his tenure a remarkable grotto was built to the Blessed Virgin. Constructed for the most part from volcanic cinders from New Mexico, it contained stones from 32 states, Canada, Mexico, and the Holy Land.

The Franciscan priests and brothers from Cincinnati, Ohio, were invited by Bishop Kelley to care for the missions of the Panhandle. They began arriving in 1943 and continued to serve the area until 1964. Besides the towns with churches, the Franciscans offered Mass at numerous isolated homes scattered throughout the vast Panhandle area.

As Guymon developed economically in the 1970's, plans were laid for a new church. The 500-seat structure, at Twelfth and North Quinn, was dedicated on April 22, 1985. It was followed by a new rectory and a paved parking lot. Social outreach programs were instituted at Guymon —a community food pantry program known as Loaves and Fishes, as well as Project Respond and the Christmas Day Dinner—as well as a religious education program with a fulltime director, and a youth organization. More recently, there have been strong parish efforts to serve the increasing numbers of Hispanic parishioners in the area.

Iowa, Sac and Fox, Shawnee and Potawatomi Lands

September 22, 1891

THREE days after Bishop Meerschaert arrived to begin his ministry in Oklahoma, the region experienced its second Land Run, when, after acreages had been allotted to each tribal member, the "surplus lands" on the reservations of the Iowa, Sac and Fox, Citizen Shawnee, and Potawatomi tribes were opened to public settlement. In the stampede that began at noon, one prospective land seeker was killed, and a number of others injured. About 20,000 persons contested for 7,000 quarter-sections, and all the land was occupied in one afternoon.

On a modern map, the newest portion of the Oklahoma Territory comprised all of Lincoln and Pottawatomie Counties, together with the eastern portions of Logan, Oklahoma, and Cleveland Counties and that part of Payne County south of the Cimarron River.

An important site in the new region of white occupancy was Sacred Heart Mission, on the Potawatomi Reserve four miles above the South Canadian River (and about six miles east of the present town of Asher). The Benedictine mission, consisting of a monastery and several schools, had existed since 1877 on land that the tribe donated in return for a church and school to be erected by the monks. Sacred Heart was, in fact, the cradle of the Catholic Faith in Oklahoma.

Sept. 22 1891

Chandler

Sacred Heart

CHANDLER ◈ *Our Lady of Sorrows*

ALTHOUGH the second land run took place as scheduled, on September 22, 1891, the surveyors had not finished their work. The quarter-section farm claims were all laid out, but the new townsites were not completed for another week, and those who were hoping for business lots in town had to wait. The townsite nearest to the western starting line was on a hill and had an abundant spring, so it drew a large crowd. The place was named to honor President Harrison's assistant secretary of the interior, George Chandler, whose home was in nearby Independence, Kansas.

Father Felix DeGrasse, O.S.B., pastor of the Guthrie parish, was the first missionary to visit Chandler. The parish developed slowly enough that three years went by before Bishop Meerschaert dedicated the first church, on November 11, 1894.

Father William Ospital, O.S.B., is recorded as having been in charge of Chandler in 1893-94. Father Edward Victor Reynolds, a diocesan priest originally from Kentucky

—he was the second priest ordained by Bishop Meerschaert— was in residence from around 1899 to 1908. By then the first church had already been destroyed by a tornado and been rebuilt. In 1917 the parish became a mission of Cushing, and then of Bristow.

The third church was begun in August 1948 and dedicated on December 19, 1949. It cost $17,000 and could seat 200. When the church was completed, Father John L. Walch was assigned as resident pastor. He built a rectory and, in 1952, a parish hall.

From 1975 to 1994 Chandler was under the care of the monks of St. Gregory's Abbey. In 1984 the 1949 church was demolished to make room for a new one, to be twice its size. Archbishop Salatka dedicated this on April 3, 1986.

HARRAH
St. Teresa

THIS Oklahoma County town began life in 1894 as Pennington, then it was known as Sweeney Bridge. Finally in 1898 it became Harrah. The first Catholic church was built in 1897 by eight Catholic families that had earlier migrated from Arkansas. Mass was offered monthly until 1907, when Father Stanislaus Lepich was appointed the first pastor. In 1923 the church burned, supposedly because the altar boys failed properly to extinguish charcoal used in the censer. The present church was built in 1925. For many years the solidly Polish Catholic members of St. Teresa's constituted one of the larger parishes in the state.

JONES ◇ *St. Robert Bellarmine*

C.G. JONES was an early Oklahoma City businessman; he had a son named Luther. Jones and Luther, two neighboring towns in northeast Oklahoma County, are named for them.

In 1948 about ten Catholic families in Jones met to organize a new parish. They met in the home of Mr. and Mrs. Marion Hopcus, whose son, Robert, had recently been killed in a motorcycle accident. With the help of Catholic Extension and much labor from the parishioners and the townspeople, St. Robert Bellarmine Church was built and was dedicated on October 18, 1948.

KONAWA
Sacred Heart

MAIL for Sacred Heart parish arrives by way of the post office in Konawa. Konawa is in Seminole County, while Sacred Heart church is a full twelve miles west, in Pottawatomie County; Konawa seems to be the nearest town that still has a post office. Sacred Heart church stands on a hill overlooking the site of the original Sacred Heart Abbey, birthplace of Oklahoma Catholicism. At first, local Catholics worshipped at the abbey itself, but after the Benedictine complex was destroyed by fire in 1901, there was need for a place to celebrate the liturgy. Until a new monastery was built in 1905, the monks worshipped in a granary, one of the few buildings standing after the fire. The "Granary Church" served the local Catholics as well, until a new parish church was built in 1914.

MC LOUD ◆ *St. Vincent de Paul*

FATHER Vincent Bednarek was a young priest, about three years ordained, when he was appointed as pastor at McLoud, in the northwest corner of Pottawatomie County. He was from Chicago, of Bohemian descent, and there were numerous Bohemian Catholics in that neighborhood. Excited at the chance to build a parish and a church, Father Bednarek led the townspeople in erecting a new church, which he named after his own patron saint. Bishop Meerschaert blessed it on November 16, 1904. Within a week, however, the young priest was dead of a heart attack. The original church was destroyed by fire in 1953, and the present church was completed the following year. For many years the McLoud parish has been in the care of the monks of St. Gregory's Abbey. One of these was the late Father Augustine Horn, O.S.B., whose name has been given to the parish center.

MEEKER ◈ *St. Michael*

S<small>T. MICHAEL</small>'s began, not in Meeker, but in the nearby settlement of Anvil. A church was built there in 1894 under the supervision of Father William Ospital, O.S.B., assistant at Purcell and pastor of Chandler. In 1904 the church building was moved to Meeker, where it stood for another 78 years. The present church was begun in the fall of 1982, and Archbishop Salatka dedicated it on May 8, 1983. Meeker has always been a mission of either Chandler or Prague.

PRAGUE ◈ *St. Wenceslaus*

T<small>HE</small> Catholic church at Prague, in the southeast corner of Lincoln County, actually began at the settlement of Keokuk Falls, about six miles south in Pottawatomie County. This was an early center of Polish and Bohemian (Czech) farmers. As early as 1891 a Polish Jesuit from Chicago, Father Francis Xavier Schulak, S.J., offered Mass for settlers in the area, and it was also served by priests from Shawnee and Chandler. A church at Keokuk Falls was built around 1900, called St. Wenceslaus, for the patron saint of Bohemia. Among the families that worshipped there was that of the young Jim Thorpe. By 1907, however, this church was no longer in service.

A post office was opened at Prague in 1901, though at first it was named Barta, after a local resident, and before that the community was known as Polanka. Vincent Martinek donated some acreage located about one and a half miles from the present town, on which was built a small church surrounded by a cemetery. This seems to have happened around 1899. Another church was built within the town in 1903, but it was destroyed by a tornado in 1919. A third church, this one larger and of brick, was begun the same year and dedicated in 1921. By 1947, however, this building too was in need of replacement.

That year Father George Johnson was appointed pastor; he brought with him a small statue of the Infant of Prague

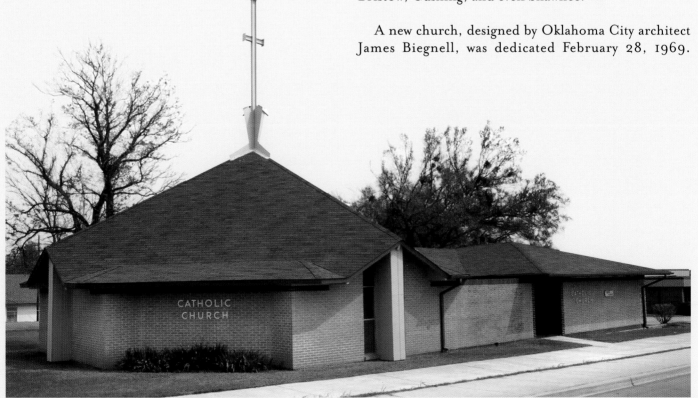

which he had been given by some nuns in California. The story goes that, as he pondered the need for a new church, he turned to the statue and asked casually, "Why don't you do something?" Before long, donations of cash, building materials, labor and talent began arriving. The building went up with the help of the parishioners and even the largely non-Catholic townspeople as well.

By this time, the great city of Prague in Czechoslovakia was behind the Iron Curtain, and the idea came to Father Johnson of putting a shrine to the Infant of Prague in the new church. Bishop McGuinness suggested that the church become a national shrine, and that is how the project developed. On the day St. Wenceslaus Church was dedicated, February 22, 1949, the National Shrine of the Infant Jesus of Prague was inaugurated as well. Pilgrimages have come to the shrine from all over Oklahoma and from every one of the 50 states. The parish now has a hundred families, but there are 4000 members in the Shrine Association.

STROUD ◆ *St. Louis*

Stroud, named for an early-day trader, was organized shortly after the Run of September 1891, and a post office opened in the fall of 1892. The parish began some ten years later, when Father E.V. Reynolds from Chandler began offering Mass in the homes of area Catholics. The first St. Louis church was built in 1901. It was named in honor of the Crusader saint and in memory of the soldiers who fell at the Battle of Gettysburg in 1863. In the years since its beginning, St. Louis parish has been under the care of pastors from Chandler, Bristow, Cushing, and even Shawnee.

A new church, designed by Oklahoma City architect James Biegnell, was dedicated February 28, 1969.

Shawnee
St. Benedict

I N 1895 Oklahoma's first east-west railroad was completed between Ft. Smith and El Reno. From Ft. Smith the Choctaw, Oklahoma, and Gulf Railroad ran southwest into the coalfields around McAlester, and then continued through Holdenville, Earlsboro, and Shawnee, before heading on to Oklahoma City. All the stops between McAlester and Oklahoma City were new towns that began in 1895 or shortly before. A post office opened in Shawnee in 1892. The railroad arrived on July 4, 1895.

The arrangement by which the Benedictines relinquished their Indian Territory prefecture assigned all the parishes in the Potawatomi Nation to the monks of Sacred Heart. The tireless Father Felix DeGrasse, O.S.B., transferred from Guthrie to Shawnee in the summer of 1895, and he supervised construction of the first church at Ninth and Park Streets. (In 1898 Father Felix was elected abbot of Sacred Heart, a post he filled until his death in January 1905.)

By 1905 the congregation had grown considerably, and because the original location was too close to a railroad, St. Benedict's people purchased the present property at Kickapoo and Benedict Streets. The cornerstone of a new church was blessed in 1906, and it was dedicated on May 12, 1907.

In 1910 the Shawnee Chamber of Commerce, wanting to have schools that would ensure the growth of the town, offered land both to the Benedictines and to the Baptists. Thus it was that St. Gregory's University and Oklahoma Baptist University were both situated west of the young city. St. Gregory's, which was briefly called the Catholic University of Oklahoma, opened its doors in September 1915.

In 1951 St. Benedict's was the scene of the funeral for the world-famous decathlon star, Jim Thorpe, prior to his interment in the town named for him in Pennsylvania. As a very young boy, Thorpe had briefly attended the school at Sacred Heart Mission.

WANETTE
St. Mary

OVER the years, the monks of Sacred Heart established missions in many of the towns of Pottawatomie County. These included Oberlin, Tecumseh, St. Gregory's Mission (variously described as situated at Eason or Trousdale), and Wanette. Of all these, only St. Mary's at Wanette has survived to the present day. A small building erected in 1897 on land belonging to a Potawatomi family named LeReau was later moved to Wanette, where it was enlarged and improved. For some years it was a center of missionary activity; the parish at Sulphur, for instance, was begun by the pastor of Wanette. At present St. Mary's is a mission of the parish of Sacred Heart, Konawa.

❖ A monastic orchestra in the Indian Territory wilderness: Sacred Heart Abbey, around 1898.
   The monk at left, with the clarinet, is artist Gregory Gerrer.

❖ Left page, bottom photo:
   The main building at St. Gregory's,
   under construction around 1914.

Cheyenne-Arapaho Reservation

April 19, 1892

THE Southern Cheyenne and Southern Arapaho tribes have been allied for many years. At the Treaty of Medicine Lodge, Kansas, in October 1867, the two groups ceded all their claims in adjoining parts of Nebraska, Kansas, Colorado, and Wyoming (except for a reserve in eastern Colorado). By a presidential proclamation of August 1869, the Arapaho and the Cheyenne were jointly assigned a reservation along the North Canadian and upper Washita Rivers, lying west from the 98th Meridian, bounded on the north by the Cherokee Outlet and on the south by the reservation of the Kiowa, Apache, and Comanche tribes

—a total of 3,500,562 acres. In 1890 the Cheyennes and Arapahoes agreed to sell this reservation to the federal government for $1,500,000, to be placed to the credit of the tribes, and with the stipulation that each tribal member receive an allotment of 160 acres. When these allotments had been made, the Cheyenne-Arapaho country was opened on April 19, 1892. About 25,000 men and women took part in this Run. Today the area includes all of Ellis, Roger Mills, and Dewey Counties, nearly all of Custer, Washita, and Blaine Counties, the north half of Beckham County, and western portions of Kingfisher and Canadian Counties.

April 19
1892

Weatherford

CALUMET
Immaculate Heart of Mary

CALUMET, in northwestern Canadian County, was named for the Native American peace pipe and established as a town site in 1893. The first Catholic church was built during the pastorate of Father Constantine Pourcin, O.S.B., of El Reno. Bishop Meerschaert dedicated the church on February 21, 1904. Nine years later, however, it was wrecked in a windstorm. Such lumber as could be salvaged was used by Father Albert Monnot, of Geary, in building the second church, dedicated to St. Anthony on October 6, 1913. A third church was dedicated to the Immaculate Heart of Mary, on April 1, 1959.

In 1941, Father Don Kanaly became pastor of Calumet. He was involved at the time in developing a correspondence school for Catholic children in parishes too small to have either a Catholic school or their own religious education program. The program moved with him to Calumet, and it was administered by two Precious Blood Sisters who resided in the town.

In recent years, the pastor of the Calumet parish has been the Catholic chaplain at the nearby U.S. Reformatory at El Reno.

The history of the parish in Calumet is linked to that of St. Joseph's in Geary, some twelve miles west in neighboring Blaine County. This parish was founded in 1912 by Father Albert Monnot. Geary, however, seems to have slipped from modern consciousness. A careful search of records, and repeated calls to possible living sources, has brought to light no further information, other than that the church, by this time a mission of Calumet, finally closed in 1977.

CLINTON
St. Mary

IT was Father Casper Douenburg, who, in 1907, four years after the founding of the town, began to conduct weekday services for the Catholics in the Clinton area. He came from Hydro. Mass was usually celebrated in the Brown Hall, on the second floor of what was afterward the Hoffman furniture store. A frame church was begun in April 1910 at Ninth and Modell, then virtually out in the country but later the center of a residential district. The church, 25 by 50 feet, was dedicated to the Blessed Virgin Mary.

Renovated in 1925, this building served until 1962 when it was replaced by the present church. St. Mary's was variously in the care of priests from Hydro, Hobart, and Geary until 1943, when Father Morris Statham was appointed the first resident pastor. He had the church moved to the 1200 block of Knox Avenue and constructed a two-story brick rectory. He also built a structure, intended as a school but always used for religious education and as a parish hall. The new St. Mary's, designed by Oklahoma City architect James Biegnell, was built at a cost of $75,000 during the pastorate of Father Sylvester H. Kleman. It opened on December 23, 1962.

CORDELL
St. Ann

IN 1906 the county seat of Washita County was moved from Cloud Chief to Cordell. That same spring, in a vacant store, Mass was celebrated in Cordell for the first time, and afterward in the homes of early parishioners. Through persistent efforts Catholics acquired property on the corner of Zada Street and Magnolia Avenue, where a pretty little brick church was started in 1906 and completed the next year with financial help of Catholic Extension. The first Mass was celebrated April 1, 1907, but its dedication to the Sacred Heart of Jesus did not take place until ten years later in 1917. In 1955 a new church was built; in May of that year it was dedicated to St. Ann.

ELK CITY
St. Matthew

Africa before coming to the United States. He arrived in Guthrie in August 1896, and Bishop Meerschaert appointed him as pastor to the wide area that encompassed everything from Mangum to Cheyenne.

Eventually he made his headquarters at Korn Valley (now Corn) in Washita County. In May 1898 he traveled 30 miles west to a part of the county's northwest corner known as Scheidel. (It was never incorporated.) He said Mass at the Tuck home, the only frame house around —all the

FOLLOWING the Cheyenne-Arapaho Run in April 1892, the eastern half of the vast tract filled quickly, but much of the western part continued for several years to be used for grazing cattle before they were shipped to the urban centers of the United States. Among those who came to farm in this cattle country were the Tucks, Schoneses, Taylors, Beckhams, and Mecheks.

Priests from El Reno brought the sacraments occasionally to these and other far-flung farmers and ranchers, but the first priest to live in the region was Father Zenon Steber, who had worked on the Gold Coast of others being dugouts. At the end of 1899 he suggested that a church be built, and the parishioners constructed one on a five acre tract donated by P.N. Schones. It was 18 by 24 feet, completed in March 1900, and named for St. Francis of Assisi. A two-room rectory addition was finished in time for the dedication the following December. In January 1901 Father Alphonse Herenthals arrived as the first resident pastor of Scheidel; he would remain for 25 years. Bishop Meerschaert came in 1906 to dedicate the second church. A separate rectory had been built, and the original church served as a parish hall. A measure of the faith of St. Francis' members may be gathered from the

＊ St. Francis, Scheidel.

fact that over the years ten women from the parish became members of religious communities.

Also in 1906, the bishop dedicated a new church, St. Joseph's, in Elk City, roughly eight miles from Scheidel, that had been built three years before. In 1911 this became a separate parish under Father Alphonse Geeraart, who served the parish until his death in 1944. He was also responsible for the missions of Sayre and Cheyenne. In 1909 Bishop Meerschaert bought the Beckham County

＊ St. Joseph's, Elk City.

＊ Holy Family, Canute.

High School and had it remodeled. It opened that year as St. Mary's Institute, staffed by the Sisters of Mercy. Since the building was separated from the church by about a mile, it was torn down in 1926 and rebuilt on donated property as St. Joseph's School.

By 1926, the nearby town of Canute had become considerably larger than Scheidel, and Holy Family parish was started there. Holy Family school opened the next year, as did the parish cemetery. A parish hall opened in 1938, and a high school ten years later. Holy Family was located right on the famous Route 66. A huge crucifixion group and a grotto were erected, which caught the attention of tourists traveling between Chicago and Los Angeles.

It was intended that St. Francis, less than three miles away, would be a mission of Canute, but the Scheidel parishioners objected so forcefully that a pastor was again assigned to Scheidel, and a school—staffed at first by the Sisters of Mercy and later by the Sisters Adorers of the Precious Blood—was built at Scheidel that operated until 1960. In that year the last resident pastor was withdrawn from Scheidel, against the continued opposition of the St. Francis parishioners. Finally, in December 1970, Bishop Victor Reed amalgamated the parishes of St. Joseph in Elk City, Holy Family in Canute, and St. Francis in Scheidel into a single new parish, St. Matthew, on the outskirts of Elk City. This was the site of St. Matthew's School, built in 1967.

It was a hard transition for parish members, who had to give up cherished church buildings to begin worshipping in temporary quarters at the school. On November 22, 1998, a permanent church was dedicated adjoining the school building. The new structure included a chapel for daily Mass, dedicated to St. Mary Magdalene.

OKARCHE
Holy Trinity

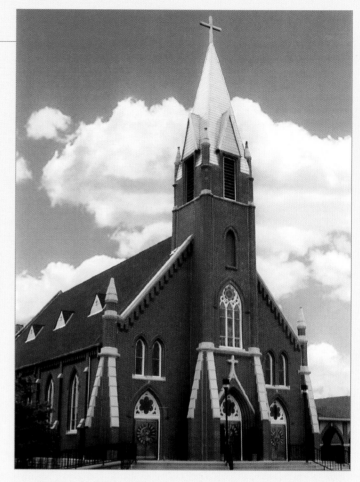

THE Okarche townsite, located one mile west of the 98th Meridian, received its first settlers the same day as the Run that opened the surplus lands of the Cheyenne-Arapaho Reservation. Its name is an amalgam of the words Oklahoma, Arapaho, and Cheyenne.

In June 1892 Father Joseph Beck, pastor of Kingfisher, began offering Mass in the homes of Okarche Catholics, most of them of German background. Because of its heavy concentration of German Catholics, Okarche would gain a reputation as "the most Catholic town in the state." Plans were quickly laid for a parish church, which opened on the feast of the Ascension, 1893. At the same time, a resident pastor was appointed, Father A.G. Borremans. Because Bishop Meerschaert was absent in Europe during much of 1893, raising money and recruiting priests, it was not until April 26, 1894, that the solemn dedication of the new church was held. Five acres of land southeast of town was donated the following year for use as a parish cemetery.

A statewide public school system was not begun in Oklahoma until 1911. From the beginning, however, Okarche Catholics were concerned for their children's education in religious and secular subjects. The first two-room school at Holy Trinity was taught by laypersons. In 1897 a two-story frame building was moved to the parish site, and Benedictine Sisters from Guthrie began teaching there, residing on the second floor while doing so. In 1903 they were replaced by the Sisters Adorers of the Most Precious Blood, from Wichita, Kansas, and in 1916 a new school building was dedicated. In 1923 high school classes were added. There was even a satellite school, St. John's, about six miles west of town, which operated from 1902 until 1918, when improved roads made its presence less necessary.

The parish saw perhaps its most significant event in November 1902, when Father Zenon Steber, who had already distinguished himself as a missionary to western Oklahoma, arrived in Okarche to begin a pastorate of 45 years that would end only with his death. Oklahomans who worry about the influx of non-English-speaking persons into the state should recall that in this period many of Okarche's Catholics spoke only German; Father Steber was from the French-German border province of Alsace, and for many years services at Okarche would be quite lengthy, for he had to preach in both English and German. With the passage of time, of course, English gradually became the language used by all parishioners.

In its first ten years, the parish had grown from twenty families to more than 125, many of the newcomers having arrived in response to advertisements in German publications. The 1893 church was now too small, and the time had come for a larger one. The bishop laid the cornerstone for this, the present church, on July 9, 1903, and it opened on the first Sunday of October.

The physical growth of Holy Trinity was matched in terms of its spiritual development, especially as measured in terms of vocations from the parish. At one point Holy Trinity was credited with more vocations to the priesthood and the sisterhoods than any other parish of its size in the Southwest, and as being among the top ranking parishes in the United States for its contributions to vocations.

Father Stanley Rother, one of nine native Okarche priests, died the death of a martyr on July 28, 1981, at the diocesan mission in Santiago Atitlan, Guatemala. His cause for beatification is now being considered by the Holy See. In 2003 a statue was erected of Father Rother as part of the centennial celebrations for the Okarche church.

In 1968, after 44 years of operation, Holy Trinity High School closed its doors. The building is now occupied by the elementary school. The parish population is over 350 families, with approximately a thousand parishioners.

OKEENE
St. Anthony of Padua

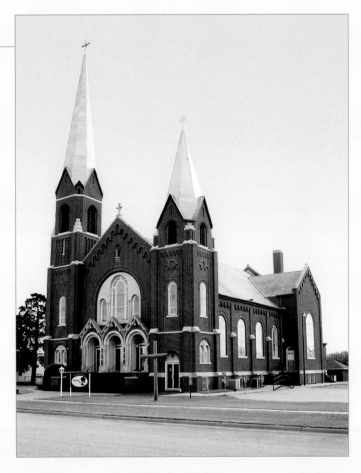

LIKE that of Okarche, Okeene's name is a composite, made up of letters from the words Oklahoma, Cherokee, and Cheyenne. The Okeene area, located in the Cimarron River valley, was illegally occupied by white men even before the 1892 Run. The townsite was occupied on the first day of the Run, but its three-days-by-wagon distance from Hennessey, the nearest town, and problems with crossing the treacherous Cimarron, did little to encourage its growth. Not until the arrival of two railroads in 1901 did Okeene begin to grow.

Bishop Meerschaert dedicated the first church on the outskirts of town in 1900. Father Urban de Hasque of Hennessey was the missionary. The first resident pastor, Father Joseph Francis Bendowski, moved the church nearer to Okeene's center, but then a violent wind moved the church from its foundations, twice in 1905 and again in 1907. The parish school opened in 1909, staffed by Benedictine Sisters from Guthrie. A large brick church was built in 1921 at a cost of $65,000; it is still in use. During the pastorate of Monsignor Paul Van Dorpe, 1938–1969, the church was known for a remarkable decorating scheme that was intended to teach lessons about the Faith. Its most renowned feature was the pulpit, which was shaped like the prow of a fishing boat, complete with nets and a life preserver that bore the legend, "S.S. Peter." An outdoor grotto dedicated to the Blessed Virgin became famous in Oklahoma clerical lore; it bore the inscription, "Hail Holy Queen, pray for Okeene."

SAYRE
Queen of All Saints

SAYRE, seat of Beckham County, became home to its first Catholic church in 1907. It was built under the direction of Father Alphonse Herenthals, who had begun offering Mass there five years earlier. Named Sacred Heart, the church was served as a mission from Scheidel and then from Elk City. The building was constructed in an unsatisfactory location, and for 20 years parishioners tried to have it moved. Finally in 1927 rollers were placed under the building and it was transported to its new location on North Fifth Street. This church stood until 1956, when it was replaced by a second structure, dedicated to the Queen of All Saints. Around 1950, Sayre became an independent parish with its own resident pastor; but in 1971 a shortage of priests led to its returning to mission status under the care of the Elk City pastor.

Sayre has been associated with St. Joseph Church in Cheyenne, in Roger Mills County, 22 miles north. Cheyenne is near the site of General Custer's famous 1869 raid on the village of the Cheyenne chief Black Kettle. St. Joseph's was built in 1924, but it has been closed since 1976.

SEILING
St. Thomas the Apostle

BISHOP McGuinness had as a personal goal to put at least one Catholic church in every county in Oklahoma. (He almost succeeded. When he died in 1957, there were only two counties, out of 77, without Catholic churches.) Seiling is in the northeast corner of Dewey County, on Highway 3 about 35 miles southeast of Woodward. Father Joseph B. McGurk, pastor of Woodward, began offering Mass in the homes of Seiling Catholics in the mid-1940's.

St. Thomas' church was originally an American Legion Hall; through the help of Seiling and Woodward parishioners half of that building was moved away and the other half turned into a church. The bishop dedicated the building in 1950.

In 1969 responsibility for Seiling was transferred to the pastor at Okeene. During the 1980's the church interior was renovated. Lastly, in 1990 a parish hall and three classrooms were attached to the church; Archbishop Salatka blessed this addition in 1991.

THOMAS
Blessed Sacrament

Thomas lies about 14 miles due east of Anthon, and the same distance north of Weatherford. Catholics there erected a small church that was dedicated to the Blessed Sacrament on February 13, 1906. Thomas existed for many years as a mission of Anthon, but in May 1949 the Anthon rectory was struck by lightning and destroyed. The pastor moved his residence to Thomas, and Anthon became the mission.

IN 1898 a number of German families settled near Anthon, in Custer County, about 25 miles northwest of Weatherford. It was in the home of Peter Klein that Father Zenon Steber, then of Korn Valley, would celebrate Mass once a month on Sunday. A four-acre tract of land was secured to serve for a church and cemetery. A building measuring 40 by 50 feet was completed on time for its dedication to Saints Peter and Paul on November 19, 1901. Anthon became an independent parish in 1908, when a small rectory was constructed.

For a few years in the 1940's, Anthon and Thomas were in the care of the pastor of Sacred Heart parish in Hinton. In 1962 Anthon was closed, and Thomas and Hinton became missions of the new parish of Weatherford.

WATONGA
St. Rose of Lima

W ATONGA, the seat of Blaine County, was for many years a place where the pastor of Geary, 18 miles to the southeast, would offer Mass on an occasional basis. In 1935 a mission church was built there. It was a small but attractive structure, faced with stucco and with a tile roof, with stained glass windows that had been imported from Germany before World War I.

It was constructed within 30 days at a cost of $3000, which was raised by parishioners in the middle of the Depression, except for a $1000 gift from Catholic Extension. Bishop Kelley dedicated it to the first saint of the Western Hemisphere, St. Rose of Lima (Peru) on March 24, 1935. It was one of the few churches Bishop Kelley was able to dedicate in that period of economic downsizing. To the north of Watonga are the former parishes of Hitchcock and Loyal. Both date from the beginning of the 20th century, but they were closed in 1997 because their congregations had dwindled in comparison with the needs of other parishes. As for St. Rose of Lima Church, in recent years it has been a mission of Okeene, but in 2004 it was transferred to the care of the pastor of Kingfisher.

WEATHERFORD ◆ *St. Eugene*

A LTHOUGH Bishop Meerschaert preached in Weatherford as early as 1902, churches were standing in the neighboring towns of Anthon, Hydro, Hinton, and Thomas years before the first place of worship was begun at Weatherford. Not until 1945 did Weatherford become designated as a mission of Blessed Virgin Church in Hydro, which had opened in 1906, the same year that the Hinton and Thomas churches were blessed.

At first Masses in Weatherford were offered on the campus of Southwestern State College. Not much space was needed, since there were only twelve Catholics in town. In 1947 an old Protestant church in Elk City was purchased and moved to South State Street; it was dedicated to St. James. By 1959 the congregation had grown to 33 members, not including about a dozen college students. Work began on a new $60,000 church in the fall of that year, and the first Masses were offered on Easter Sunday, 1960. In 1962 the priest from Hydro was transferred to Weatherford; Hydro continued as a mission of Weatherford until 1965 when it was closed.

It is likely that St. Eugene Church was built in memory of Bishop Eugene McGuinness, who had died not long before. Besides being Oklahoma's bishop for thirteen years, McGuinness earlier had been vice president of the Extension Society, and Extension had contributed toward the construction. In 1983 the parish built a parish hall, and in 1997 Archbishop Beltran dedicated a new religious education building with office space and an area for the St. Vincent de Paul Society.

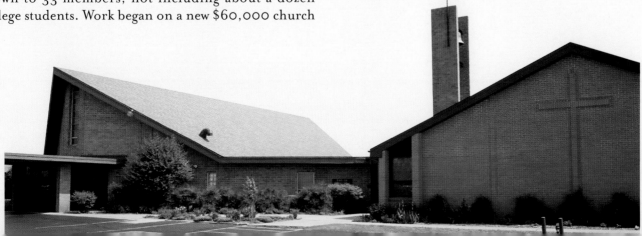

The Cherokee Outlet

September 16, 1893

THE Cherokee Outlet —not to be confused with the Cherokee Strip, which is in Kansas and is the result of a surveying error— was originally set aside in 1825 as hunting grounds for Cherokees that were uncomfortable with their new homeland in the eastern portion of the Indian Territory. Over the years, the Cherokees sold off portions of this 3,000,000-acre tract to other tribes, especially to the Osages, but it remained a very large region, about as long as the Panhandle and nearly twice as wide. When it was opened for settlement on September 16, 1893, about 100,000 persons made the Run, making this the greatest of all five land runs. On the same day, an additional 169,000 acres, formerly belonging to the Pawnee tribe and adjacent to the Cherokee Outlet, as well as 79,000 acres that had been the property of the Tonkawas, was opened to white settlement. At statehood in 1907, eight counties, and the greater parts of three others, would be created from this area.

It is worth noting that several groups of Plains Indians were settled in the Cherokee Outlet after 1870, most of them in what eventually became Kay and Osage Counties. The government purchased reservation lands for them from the Cherokees, or else the agents assigned to the tribes negotiated these sales. Besides the Osages, these included the Kaws, the Poncas, the Nez Perce —who actually managed to return to their homeland; their reservation was afterward acquired by the Tonkawas— and the Otoe-Missourias. Except in the case of the Osages, no Catholic church was ever built within any of these reservation boundaries.

Sept. 16
1893

•Enid

ALVA
Sacred Heart

THE Alva area was so far removed from the first settlements in the Cherokee Outlet that it was a priest from Wichita, Kansas, who offered the first Mass there in 1895. Father Renier Sevens, pastor of Pond Creek, organized the Alva parish in 1897. By 1899 a church was standing at Fourth and Choctaw, and Father Charles Standaert was appointed first resident pastor.

From 1933 to 1961, Father Leo Claus was pastor. He oversaw construction of the present church in 1937, a town landmark. Bishop Kelley dedicated it on November 9, 1937. The parish school operated from 1927 to 1966.

BLACKWELL ❖ *St. Joseph*

ALTHOUGH Mass was offered in the Blackwell area as early as 1894, it was not until the spring of 1901 that the first church was built and the first services held there. Father Renier Sevens, then of Ponca City, oversaw construction and celebrated Mass. In 1905 St. Joseph's became an independent parish with its own resident pastor. This arrangement continued until 1926, when the pastor at that time, Father Edward Mallen, moved his residence to a new rectory in Tonkawa,

❖ The 1901 church

about nine miles distant. A new St. Joseph's was built in 1939 and dedicated that year on October 25, with Bishop Kelley presiding.

Because of the close proximity of Blackwell and Tonkawa, and the shortage of priests, the same priest has generally been in charge of both places, with his rectory in one or the other as circumstances have dictated. At present, the pastor lives in Blackwell.

BILLINGS
Sacred Heart

Father Willebrord Voogden, O.S.B, pastor of Perry, was the first priest to celebrate Mass in a farm house two miles south of Billings in 1895. Services may have been held occasionally in or near the town by the priest of Ponca City; but from 1899 Billings was attended from Hennessey, and three years later with the appointment of a resident priest at Enid, Billings was visited regularly by the assistant pastor there. In 1901, Father Urban de Hasque, of Hennessey, came once a month to Billings to offer Mass in the Woodmen's or Odd Fellows hall and on the following morning celebrated Mass in the home of a Mr. Mennehan. In 1906 the congregation bought the former Methodist church in Billings, added a sanctuary, and transformed the pulpit into a confessional. Other renovations and improvements were made later. The building remains in regular use as a mission of Perry.

BISON
St. Joseph

Bison lies along the Rock Island line between Hennessey and Enid. The parish was comprised mainly of Czech farmers, and it was a Czech-speaking priest from Hennessey, Father Joseph Sinkmajer, who first visited them in 1904. Father Sinkmajer did not remain long in the Oklahoma Territory, however; another Czech-speaking priest, Father Joseph Lusar, the pastor at Yukon, also paid visits to the Catholics around Bison, and it was he, in 1908, that obtained the first pledges toward a church. This was constructed the next year on donated land, and Bishop Meerschaert presided at its dedication to St. Joseph on October 14, 1909. A school and a rectory soon followed, and in 1912, Father Hector Schaubroeck became the first resident pastor. Sisters of Divine Providence operated the school until 1934, when they were succeeded by Sisters Adorers of the Most Precious Blood. The school closed in 1967.

Father Andrew Thomas was in the parish only briefly, but he was responsible for obtaining for St. Joseph's the diocesan shrine of Our Lady of Fatima, dedicated in 1951. The Fatima cult was strong among American Catholics for many years, and numerous parishes sent annual pilgrimages to Bison. The shrine was destroyed by an electrical fire resulting from a storm in 1992, but it was rebuilt and Archbishop Beltran dedicated it on October 30, 1994. The Bison parish has given the Church four priests and six religious sisters.

BUFFALO

St. Joseph

ARPER COUNTY marks the point where the Oklahoma Panhandle joins the remainder of the state. Buffalo, established in 1907, is the county seat and almost the only town. The first Catholic church was a frame building constructed in 1909 during the pastorate of Father Peter Kamp of Woodward. The principal donor was Mr. Joseph Roetker, in whose honor the church was named for St. Joseph. It was never officially dedicated. In 1930 it was replaced by a larger brick church. The interior was largely unfinished, but by 1945 this work was done, and Bishop McGuinness dedicated the building on November 26, 1945. From 1947 to 1978 Buffalo was an independent parish, but for most of its history it has been attended from Woodward, some 35 miles to the southeast.

CHEROKEE

St. Cornelius

ATHER Cornelius Smeur was born in The Netherlands, was ordained there in 1900, and arrived in Oklahoma in 1903. He was immediately appointed pastor of Alva, and he continued in that post until his death in 1927. A very active missionary, he tended churches in Capron, Cherokee, Carmen, Milan, Syria, and Waynoka in Woods county, and Woodward, Mooreland, Curtis, Gage, Fort Supply, and Quinlan in Woodward County.

Father Renier Sevens said the first Mass at Cherokee in 1899 in the home of Jacob and Anna Brown. In 1904 Father Smeur purchased a former schoolhouse and had it moved to property that the congregation had already purchased. Bishop Meerschaert blessed St. Cornelius Church on February 2, 1906. At the time, the parish had just twelve members.

The present brick church was built in 1930 with a capacity of 300. By 1954 the congregation had grown to 50 families. Father Richard Dolan became the first resident pastor in 1954, and he built the rectory and the parish hall. Although today Cherokee is again being attended from Alva, it has its own permanent deacon.

ENID
St. Francis Xavier

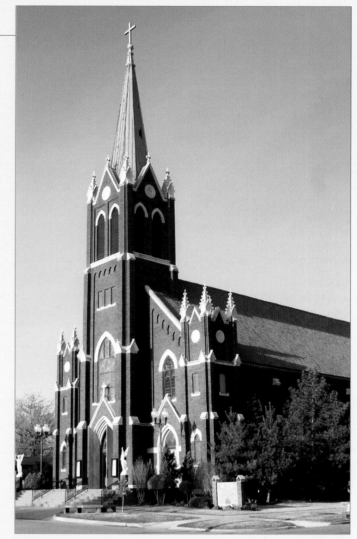

FATHER Joseph Beck, pastor of Hennessey on the Rock Island line, offered the first Mass in the new town of Enid. This took place in the home of Hugh Johnson, with seventeen Catholics present. This would be more or less the pattern in Enid for the next several years. As late as 1897, when Bishop Meerschaert came for Confirmation, the ceremony had to be held at the opera house because there was no church. That year, however, the bishop appointed his own nephew, Father Gustave Depreitere, as missionary to the region; but Father Depreitere was stationed down the tracks at Hennessey, where he was also pastor.

In 1899 he purchased lots on the block bounded by Broadway, Madison, Monroe, and Randolph streets. There he built the first Catholic church in Enid, which Bishop Meerschaert dedicated in honor of St. Francis Xavier, patron of missions, on May 1, 1900. A year later, Father Depreitere became the first resident pastor of the parish. In 1904 St. Joseph's School was opened in a two-story red brick building on Randolph. Five Sisters of Divine Providence came from San Antonio, Texas, to teach in the school. The custom of these sisters was to operate a school of twelve grades, so from an early time St. Francis Xavier had a high school.

When the Diocese of Oklahoma was established in 1905, the primary change was from a loosely-organized structure of governance, centered on a traveling bishop, to a more formal one with a central chancery. One of the appointments required in the diocesan arrangement was of a vicar general, an official somewhat like a lieutenant governor who could act in the bishop's stead when the latter was out of the diocese. The bishop's choice to fill the post was Father Depreitere. In the early years he was able to perform his duties while living in Enid, but in 1919 he transferred to Oklahoma City. His replacement was Father Renier Sevens, already noted as a builder; it was he who oversaw construction of the new church, which was dedicated on May 27, 1922. The building has continued in use until the present.

Events of special interest in the ensuing years included the 1949 renaming of the Enid Air Field for Lt. Col. Robert L. Vance, a St. Francis Xavier parishioner who received the Congressional Medal of Honor. Also of note was the appointment of Msgr. Stephen A. Leven, pastor of St. Francis Xavier, as auxiliary bishop of San Antonio in 1955.

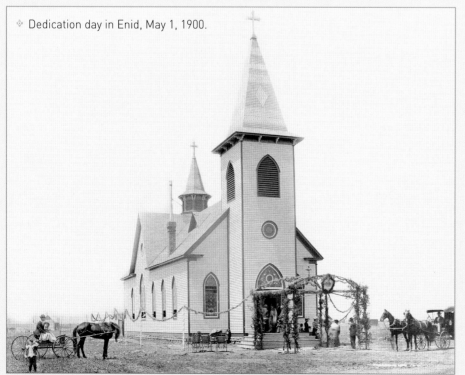

⬥ Dedication day in Enid, May 1, 1900.

ENID
St. Gregory the Great

ENID's second parish was established in September 1971, with Father Robert Siebs as the first pastor. Growth of the city toward the north inspired the development of the new pastoral area, which included the town of Kremlin. The creation of this parish was one of Bishop Reed's last official acts; he suffered a stroke and died just after midnight on September 8. At first, Mass was offered in the Enid Knights of Columbus hall. At one of the first parish meetings, the members voted to name the parish in honor of Pope St. Gregory VII, called the Great for his enormous influence in his own day, the eleventh century. Father Siebs was transferred in 1972 and was replaced by Father Larry Gatlin, who oversaw fundraising and construction of the new church. Archbishop Quinn presided at its dedication on July 13, 1974.

FAIRVIEW
St. Ann

FAIRVIEW is the seat of Major County. Mass was first offered there in 1915, possibly by Father Joseph Francis (Bendowski) of Okeene. In the years that followed, Fairview Catholics celebrated the Eucharist more or less regularly, usually once a month. In November 1948, however, Bishop McGuinness established St. Ann's, which was placed in charge of the pastor at Goltry. The church, which seats 120 people, was built in 1950. Today St. Ann's is attended from Okeene.

GOLTRY
St. Michael

GOLTRY, in Alfalfa County, became a parish in 1912. It was the project of Father Gustave Depreitere, of Enid, and Father Alfred Deckmyn, his assistant, became the first resident pastor. With the outbreak of World War I in 1914, however, the French government called home all its male citizens, including priests, to contribute to the war effort. Father Deckmyn returned to France in 1915 and served in the French army as a chaplain. He survived the war but did not return to the United States.

A school opened at Goltry in 1920. On June 1, 1926, St. Michael's Church was destroyed by fire; this led to the present graceful brick structure designed by Harold Gemeno of Norman, who was also responsible for the Mater Admirabilis university chapel in that city (page 62). When St. Gregory the Great parish opened in Enid in 1971, Goltry was attached to it as a mission.

In 1951 the pastor was Father Bernard Havlik of Goltry. He conceived the idea of opening a church at Ringwood, eleven miles south in Major County. The diocese purchased a small bank building, 25 feet wide by 50 feet long, and Catholic Extension contributed funds to remodel it. The Extension donor placed as a condition that the church be named for St. Ethlebert. In spite of the best efforts of the few Catholic families in Ringwood, however, St. Ethlebert's mission was not very successful. It closed in 1968.

MEDFORD
St. Mary

to Manchester where, on the 15th, at a spot six miles from town, he blessed Ss. Peter and Paul Church. Two days later he dedicated St. Anthony's at Clyde. These were rural churches built to be near the farm families they served.

In contrast, Medford, the county seat, was slow to attract Catholics, at least in numbers sufficient to justify a fifth parish in western Grant County. Eventually, however, the great demographic shift in the U.S. from country to town and city meant that the frame church north of Numa had to be moved ten miles to Medford. This occurred on June 6, 1940, after which the building was remodeled and opened for services. A new church was built in 1948-49 and dedicated by Bishop McGuinness on May 10, 1949. Medford was then given the missions of Pond Creek and Clyde.

NUMA, in Grant County, is little more than a rail siding today, but in the 1890's it had its own post office. The original St. Mary's Church was built in a place even more remote, some three and a half miles north of Numa. Father Renier Sevens, then of Pond Creek, built this church and Bishop Meerschaert presided at its dedication on September 13, 1898. The next day he traveled

MOORELAND
Sacred Heart

WHEN the post office was established here in 1902, the citizens, having decided that the surrounding prairie expanses were reminiscent of the moors of Yorkshire, applied to have their town named Moorland. But, as often happened, mistakes were made in Washington, and the application was returned with "Mooreland" as the approved name. The first Catholic church in Mooreland, eleven miles east of Woodward, was originally a school building in that town. Father Cornelius Smeur, pastor of Alva, bought it and had it moved to Lot 11 in Block 1 of the Knittel addition to Mooreland. Father Peter Kamp, appointed first resident pastor of Woodward in early 1905, had it remodeled. During his pastorate it was dedicated to St. Joseph on February 5, 1906. By the mid-1930's, most of the Catholics in Quinlan, nine miles east of Mooreland, had moved from the town. The church in Quinlan, built in 1917, was closed and in 1934 the structure was moved in sections to Mooreland to become the second church there. Since the Quinlan church had been dedicated to the Sacred Heart, that name was retained in Mooreland.

NEWKIRK
St. Francis of Assisi

NEWKIRK, ten miles north of Ponca City, is the county seat of Kay County. Originally named Lamereux, it then became Santa Fe, before receiving its present name, which was chosen to distinguish it from a former rail stop two miles north that was called Kirk.

The first Catholic services after the opening of the Cherokee Outlet were held in the home of Mrs. John Smith. Later a frame commercial structure was bought at Cross (now a part of Ponca City) for $150.00. With the help of mules and a steam engine, it was moved to the corner of Eighth Street and Magnolia Avenue in Newkirk, to be used as a temporary church. In 1898 Father Renier Sevens of Pond Creek, with the aid of $500.00 from the Catholic Church Extension Society and contributions from the members of the congregation, built a new church on Main Street at an original cost of $1,500.00. It was dedicated on August 24, 1898. In 1907, however,

the entire 600 block on West Ninth Street was purchased for about $1800.00, and in 1910 the church was moved to that location.

In 1906 Father John Kekeisen was named first resident pastor. He opened a school, in which he and his unmarried sister taught until the first teaching sisters arrived in 1910. In 1953 Bishop McGuinness dedicated a new church, and in 1954 a new rectory and convent were built, followed by a new school building in 1961.

PERRY
St. Rose of Lima

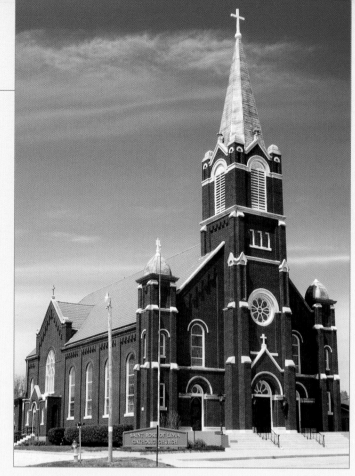

ACCORDING to the *Annals of Sacred Heart Abbey*, Father Leo Gariador, O.S.B., visited Perry the day it opened, September 16, 1893. It appears, however, that the first time Mass was celebrated at Perry was on October 31, when Father A.G. Borremans, the assistant to Father Felix DeGrasse at Guthrie, offered the Eucharist in the back room of a grocery store. He also presided at a double wedding that day.

Less than a year later Bishop Meerschaert dedicated a new church in Perry to St. Rose of Lima, a patron chosen by members of the parish altar society. The date was August 26, 1894. The following January, a Benedictine priest named Father Willibrord Voogden, O.S.B., who was serving as pastor at Ponca City, took on Perry as a mission, and soon after, he was named resident pastor there, continuing a pastorate that would last thirty-six years. The present St. Rose of Lima Church dates from 1923; its dedication on October 24 was Bishop Meerschaert's last formal appointment before his final illness and death.

The parish opened a cemetery in 1898, and St. Joseph's Academy opened on September 8, 1900, with 175 students. The Sisters of Divine Providence comprised the faculty; it was the first mission in Oklahoma for this Texas-based community, which over the years would send more than 850 sisters to teach in Oklahoma's parochial schools. Sisters Adorers of the Most Precious Blood provided instruction in St. Joseph's school from the mid-1950's. St. Joseph's academy and high school closed in 1935, and the elementary school closed in 1968.

In 1977 the church underwent a thorough renovation. One of the highlights of this project was the acquisition of bronze doors at the main entrance. Part of the copper used in the bronze was comprised of pennies, gathered by two families chiefly responsible for having the doors made and installed.

PONCA CITY
St. Mary

✧ Interior of St. Mary's, Ponca City, showing dramatic statue of the Risen Christ.

AMONG the townsites that opened at the Cherokee Outlet Run, those adjacent to the right-of-way of the Santa Fe Railroad were destined to develop early and fast. This was true of the Catholic parishes in those towns as well.

Father Felix DeGrasse, O.S.B., was pastor of Guthrie, with responsibility for towns along the Santa Fe line. It is not known just when he made his first visit to Ponca City, but it was probably within a month of the opening, because the cornerstone of a new frame church was laid in November 1893, on land donated by Mr. and Mrs. Michael Daley, whose daughter would be the first child baptized in the completed building. This first church was dedicated to St. Felix, in honor of Father DeGrasse's patron. He offered the first Mass on March 17, 1894, and Bishop Meerschaert presided at the formal dedication on May 26. A second church, larger and built of brick, was dedicated to St. Mary on October 15, 1916.

Because of the scarcity of priests at the time, there was considerable turnover of pastors for the first several years. In 1900, however, Father Renier Sevens, ordained in 1896, was assigned to Ponca City; he remained for thirteen years and contributed substantially to the development, not only of the Ponca City parish, but of several others as well. One of his first tasks was the creation of St. Mary's Academy, which opened in 1901. By 1912 it had an enrollment of 200 in twelve grades. A second school building, two stories high and made of brick, was

constructed in 1928; it was located several blocks from the church, and it was on this property that the third and present church would be built in 1954. This lovely structure, built in a modified Italian Renaissance style, has been the subject of continued improvements over the years. It presently features a monumental statue of the Risen Christ, of wood glowing with gold leaf, that floats above the main altar and dominates the interior.

In 1941 the magnificent estate of Ponca City oilman E.W. Marland came into the possession of the Carmelite Fathers, who used it as a priory and novitiate. In 1948 the property passed to the Felician Sisters, who established Assumption Villa, a provincial motherhouse. This included a high school for girls wishing to enter the order. The high school at St. Mary's parish was experiencing a downturn in enrollment, and the suggestion was made that the two high schools pool their resources. The result was Unity High, with an ecumenical board of directors. It operated from 1968 to 1971.

In 1988, St. Mary's initiated a housing ministry with six units, making them available to low-income elderly parishioners at a reduced rental. The parish, which earlier had as many as 2000 parishioners, presently counts 838, the result of the merger of Conoco-Phillips and the consequent departure of many families connected with the oil business.

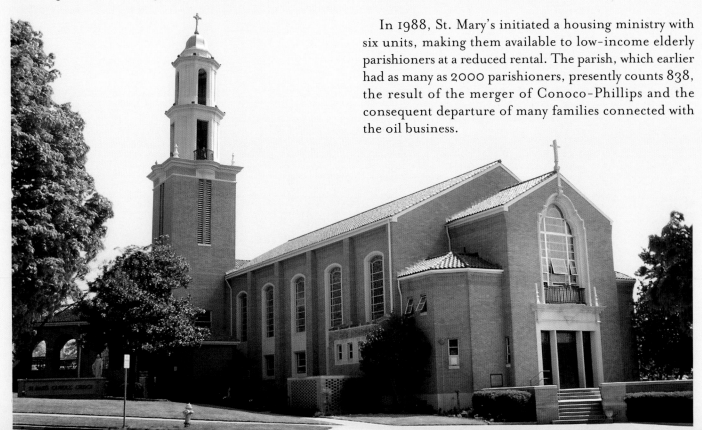

POND CREEK
St. Joseph

1893 Run; this was also a stop on the railroad. Difficulties between the Rock Island executives and the town, however, caused the rail station to be moved three miles south. The new location was called Pond Creek, and the original site became Jefferson.

It was to Jefferson that Father Joseph Beck, pastor of Hennessey, first came in 1895. He offered Mass in the home of the Glahn family. Eventually he decided that Pond Creek was the more favorable location for a church, and St. Joseph's was built there in 1896. Bishop Meerschaert appointed Father Renier Sevens as first resident pastor in 1897, and the bishop dedicated the church on May 25, 1898. Father Sevens was transferred to Ponca City in 1900, and his successor would be the last resident pastor in Pond Creek. From 1904 to the present, Pond Creek has been a mission successively of Hennessey, of Enid, and currently of Medford. A new St. Joseph's was built in 1949.

THE Rock Island Railroad began building south through the Indian Territory around 1888. By the time of the 1889 Land Run, the tracks were laid as far south as Hennessey. The railroad followed approximately the 98th Meridian, along the line of the Chisholm Trail, which it was intended to replace.

A post office was established on the Rock Island at a place called Round Pond less than two weeks after the

SHATTUCK ◇ Holy Name

SHATTUCK, in Ellis County, lies approximately 32 miles southwest of Woodward. Construction of a church there began in September 1905. It was a frame building costing about $1000.00. Father Peter Kamp, pastor of Woodward, offered the first Mass in November. The church was named for St. James the Apostle, apparently because James Tagney was the chair of the building committee. When Buffalo became a parish in 1947,

Shattuck was assigned to it as a mission. In 1949 the first Glenmary Home Missioner in Oklahoma, Father John Marquardt, was assigned to Buffalo and Shattuck. In 1955 Father Marquardt built a new church in Shattuck. On May 31, 1955, Bishop McGuinness dedicated the new structure to the Holy Name of Jesus. In this he was, presumably, honoring the wishes of a donor who had contributed funds for the church through Catholic Extension.

TONKAWA
St. Joseph

THE first Catholic church in Tonkawa started life as a Methodist place of worship. In 1909 Father Renier Sevens, then pastor of Ponca City, bought the church on behalf of the Catholics in Tonkawa. Bishop Meerschaert blessed it for Catholic use on May 3, 1909. It was not uncommon in turn-of-the-century Oklahoma for buildings to be recycled in this fashion.

Father Sevens had been involved with Tonkawa Catholics since 1903. After 1911, however, Tonkawa was a mission of Blackwell. But Tonkawa was also the center of the Three Sands oil boom in the 1920's, and the area farmers and merchants, Catholics among them, were becoming rich from the oil leases they owned. It seemed to be time for a new church in Tonkawa.

The pastor in Blackwell at the time was Father Edward Mallen. It fell to him to superintend construction of a new brick structure. Bishop Kelley laid the cornerstone on October 20, 1925. When the church was finished, Father Mallen moved to Tonkawa, and Blackwell became the mission parish.

Because money was not a problem, the church was paid for almost as soon as it was completed. This created an unusual opportunity. In those days, a church could be dedicated, but not consecrated, before it was debt-free. Since St. Joseph's had no debt, it could be inaugurated with the full panoply of Catholic ritual, in a service that ordinarily took six hours. It happened that Bishop Kelley was entertaining a houseguest from Rome at his residence in Oklahoma City, and so Archbishop Joseph Palica was drafted to conduct the ceremony, with Bishop Kelley assisting. The marathon ceremony took place on July 5, 1926. For obvious reasons, consecrated churches have

been a rarity in Oklahoma. St. Joseph's in Tonkawa is one of the few in the state, at least prior to Vatican II, as a result of which the ceremony was drastically shortened and applied to all new churches.

When Bishop Kelley was a young priest, he was the pastor of a small parish in rural Michigan. He reasoned that, if several priests could live in a central location, they could spread the ministry among themselves, cover a greater territory, and also combat the loneliness and intellectual isolation that country pastors often have to contend with. There was a new rectory at Tonkawa, and it was big enough to serve as a laboratory for the bishop's experiment. Although it was tried in a few other Oklahoma towns, Tonkawa was where it had its greatest success, especially under the dynamic Father Stephen Leven, who was one of the most fervent missionaries the Oklahoma Church ever knew.

In 1948 the parish opened an elementary school staffed by the Felician Sisters, whose motherhouse at the time was in nearby Ponca City. Like so many struggling rural school, however, this one had to close its doors in 1963.

✧ The original St. Joseph's, Tonkawa, a former Methodist church.

WAKITA
St. Mary
Assumption

WAKITA, in Grant County, is a mission of Medford. Its post office was established in 1893. Wakita is a Cherokee word; it refers to water collected in a depression, such as a buffalo wallow. The parish began in 1947 when Father Urban de Hasque, at the time pastor at Manchester, purchased a former Protestant church and hall and remodeled them for Catholic use. Bishop McGuinness performed the dedication ceremony on May 30, 1948. In 1952, Father Vytautas Zakaras, a Lithuanian priest who had succeeded Father de Hasque at Manchester, built a rectory in Wakita and became the first resident pastor. The parish became a mission of Medford on June 15, 1988.

WAYNOKA
Our Mother of Mercy

As the crow flies, Waynoka, in Woods County, is twenty miles southwest of Alva, whose pastor also serves Waynoka. (Waynoka is a Cheyenne word meaning "sweet water.") In the 1920's most of the Catholics in Waynoka were Mexican nationals working for the Santa Fe railroad. In those days fruit from California was carried east in iced container cars, and Waynoka was one of the points where the ice was replenished. The priest at Alva did not speak Spanish, and providing pastoral leadership was a problem until Father Mariano Gutierrez, exiled from his home diocese of Chilocco by the Mexican revolution, arrived in Alva in 1928. Our Mother of Mercy Church was built in 1931, and Father Gutierrez moved to Waynoka. His health broke in 1935, but he was replaced by another Mexican priest, who remained about a year. By this time the technology for shipping fruit had improved to the point that icing was no longer necessary, and most of Waynoka's Catholics were assigned to other places by the railroad. Those who remained were served by Spanish-speaking priests of a Franciscan community in Wichita Falls, Texas, from 1936 to 1952.

WOODWARD

St. Peter

Father Kamp's church, named for his patron saint, stood until April 9, 1947, when it was destroyed in one of the most ferocious tornadoes ever to strike the Sooner State. The F5 storm began near Canadian, in the center of the Texas Panhandle, and traveled continuously on the ground for over a hundred miles, producing sixty-nine fatalities before crossing into Oklahoma. It was nearly two miles wide, with forward speeds of up to fifty miles an hour. In Woodward, over a hundred city blocks on the west and north sides of the city were destroyed. Confusion and fires reigned in the aftermath with over a thousand homes and businesses destroyed, at least 107 people killed in and around Woodward, and nearly a thousand additional injuries. Normal communications between Woodward and the outside world were not restored for some time and there was great uncertainty as to the status of victims. The Woodward tornado was one of the chief reasons for the National Weather Service's establishing a tornado watch and warning program in 1953.

Because of the devastation, the parishioners at St. Peter's found it impossible to rebuild for some time. A Quonset hut served as a church in Woodward for over ten years, but eventually funds were raised and construction begun. Bishop Victor Reed blessed the new St. Peter's on November 22, 1960. The church was soon followed by a new education building and parish hall.

St. Peter's has long been the center of mission activity for priests working in northwest Oklahoma. Parishes at Buffalo, Mooreland, Shattuck, and Beaver are currently served from Woodward, and Quinlan was also a mission until it closed a few years ago. Western State Hospital and Corrections Department at Fort Supply is another focus of ministry in the area.

THE centennial year of the Archdiocese of Oklahoma City also is the one hundredth anniversary of St. Peter parish in Woodward. On January 28, 1905, Father Peter Kamp, who was stationed at Alva with his cousin, Father Cornelius Smeur, received a letter from Bishop Meerschaert that appointed him first pastor of Woodward, with instructions to begin constructing a church.

In fact, however, mission activity in the Woodward area dates at least to 1872, because that year Father Paul Ponziglione, S.J., visited the nearby Army garrison at Camp Supply. Father Ponziglione was stationed at St. Paul, Kansas, not far from the Missouri border, from 1851 to 1889, but he was an inveterate traveler who toured all the parishes of southern Kansas and as far south as Fort Sill. Father Ferdinand Wolf, O.S.B., from Atchison, Kansas, also ministered occasionally at Camp Supply. Woodward developed as a townsite because it was the nearest point at Camp Supply (later called Fort Supply) on the railroad.

❖ The Woodward church and rectory, destroyed by a tornado in 1947.

Kickapoo Lands

IN the 17th century, the Kickapoo tribe had its home in the region of southern Wisconsin. In the 1830's the tribe was relocated to northeastern Kansas, and in 1871 they began moving to the Indian Territory. The Kickapoos, considerably reduced in numbers, were assigned a reservation on lands that had been part of the Creek Nation, between the Deep Fork and the North Canadian Rivers, with the Sac and Fox lands to their east and the Unassigned Lands on their west. Always independent, the Kickapoos had not yet agreed to the terms offered for their surplus lands when the second Land Run was conducted in 1891. Nearly four years elapsed before their small reservation was opened to white settlement. After tribal members received allotments totaling 22,640 acres, some 200,000 acres were opened on May 23, 1895. Today the Kickapoos are mostly to be found in and around McLoud, in Pottawatomie County.

At the present time, no Catholic parishes are located within the boundaries of the former Kickapoo reservation. The town of Luther lies just south of the Deep Fork, and St. Therese church therefore stood on land that had belonged to the Kickapoos. But in 2002 that church was moved to Our Lady of the Lake Lodge near Guthrie to serve as a chapel; it was renamed in honor of St. Katharine Drexel.

May 23 1895

•Shawnee

Greer County

March 16, 1896

WHEN the United States made the Louisiana Purchase from France in 1803, no one was sure precisely how much territory was included or even where the boundaries were. It was generally agreed, however, that the Red River comprised part of that boundary. The question was whether the main stream of the river followed its northern or its southern fork. Texas claimed that its territory was bounded by the North Fork of the Red, but this claim was contested by the Oklahoma Territory government. In 1896 the issue was settled by the U.S. Supreme Court in favor of Oklahoma, and Old Greer County —as the area between the branches of the Red was known— became officially part of the Oklahoma Territory. Since the area had not been assigned to any native tribe, and since it was already partially occupied, no land run was held to open it. Today the region comprises all of Jackson, Harmon, and Greer Counties, and the southern half of Beckham County.

March 16 1896

•Mangum

ALTUS
Prince of Peace

ATHER Willem Huffer, pastor of Lawton, offered the first Mass in Altus in 1906. By 1909 Father Alphonse Geeraert of Mangum was saying Mass in Altus once a month. In 1914 he purchased a house, which was used as a church until 1926, when Father Louis Hugo bought the old Church of Christ and had it moved to 901 East Liveoak Street; he titled the church St. Sophie Magdalen. St. Madeleine Sophie Barat (1779-1865) was the foundress of the Madames of the Sacred Heart. She had just been canonized in 1925.

The parish's first home was replaced twenty years later when the Altus Air Field closed in 1946 and the old base chapel was available. The Little family made the purchase possible. In 1954 the Air Force Base reopened, and there was a new surge of Catholics among the workers there. By 1962 the need for a new church and a parish was imperative, and Bishop Reed appointed Father Philip Bryce as Altus' first resident pastor. He bought ten acres on the northeast side of town, and the new Prince of Peace Church was built. Bishop Reed blessed it on December 3, 1964.

The second Catholic explosion in Altus occurred when Mexican migrant workers began arriving to work in the cotton fields. Father Bryce organized parishioners to distribute food, clothing, and financial assistance.

In 1969 Sophia Hall was dedicated with seven classrooms for religious education classes. Ten years later a wing was built with added classrooms, and the whole facility was renamed the Father Stanley F. Rother Center. The parish has known continued growth, with 84 baptisms in 1978 alone; half of these were of Mexican-American infants.

HOLLIS
Our Lady of Guadalupe

Durdeyns. They were accompanied by a sudden influx of about 2,000 Mexican workers who had been hired to pick cotton. Dominican priests from Mangum said Mass in the home of the Macias family, and later in a local movie theatre. In 1957 the Legion of Mary was started under the patronage of Our Lady of Guadalupe. Legion members found themselves working to alleviate the terrible living conditions the migrant laborers and their families had to endure. One of the Dominicans located a prefabricated building in Minneapolis, and Bishop Reed paid to have the structure moved to Hollis and set up on property the congregation had purchased for $500.00. Our Lady of Guadalupe Church was dedicated by Bishop Reed on June 12, 1960. A larger, permanent church and parish hall was built in 1985.

OLLIS, the seat of Harmon County, dates to 1901, but the first Catholic, so far as is known, did not arrive until 1937. This was Genevieve Charlton, recently married and a graduate of St. Elizabeth's mission school in Purcell. For years she prayed that more Catholics would come and make a parish possible at Hollis. In 1950 two English-speaking families did come, the Bolls and the

MANGUM
Sacred Heart

FATHER Zenon Steber entered the world as a native of Alsace, a province on the French-German border. Father Zenon Steber was ordained a priest for the African missions in 1893 at the very young age of 22. His first assignment called for him to serve in the steamy Gold Coast of West Africa. His African career was cut short when he became ill, probably with yellow fever. Father Steber turned to America and contacted Bishop Meerschaert, asking to work in "new and hard missions where all is to be started." Barely five months after the Supreme Court decision that attached Greer County to the Oklahoma Territory, Father Steber arrived at Guthrie. In his diary, Bishop Meerschaert noted, "I sent him to Greer County. Gave him a buggy [and] two ponies and his missionary valise. Those were all his possessions. On his first trip to Greer County he baptized Mr. and Mrs. Shadden... and one of their daughters. On the second trip two other daughters were also baptized." The bishop later wrote that Father Steber told him the settlers of the southwestern area "live in caves or dugouts, very poor, living mostly on corn. He finds that the poverty of that country is awful and that his blacks of South Africa were living as princes compared to those people."

In 1902 a young priest with a German accent arrived in Mangum. This was Father Willem Huffer, the pastor at Lawton. His mission was to encourage and oversee the construction of a Catholic church in Mangum. Bishop Meerschaert dedicated the new white frame church to the

Sacred Heart of Jesus on December 6, 1902. In 1908 the bishop assigned Mangum's first resident pastor; Father Alphonse Geeraert was a Belgian missionary to America, well educated at the University of Louvain. He was 27 years old when he arrived in Greer County. The young priest had no way to know it then, but in God's providence he was to spend the remainder of his life, thirty-six years, along the western border of Oklahoma in Mangum and Elk City. During his pastorate a choir loft, a steeple, and a 1,600-pound bell were added to Sacred Heart Church.

At statehood, "Greer County" was divided into three new counties. The pastor of Mangum became responsible for a mission church at Hollis, and eventually for Hobart, Altus, and Frederick as well.

From 1911 to 1926 Mangum was a mission of Elk City with Father Geeraert as its pastor. Father Louis Hugo was assigned in early 1926 to build and operate a mission center at Sacred Heart Church. He thus became the second resident pastor at Mangum.

Bishop Kelley had taken office two years earlier following the death of Bishop Meerschaert. He had an imaginative plan for the great reaches of his diocese in which he did not have enough priests. His idea was to build a larger than usual rectory and to assign several priests there to serve a wide area. This would help the priests plan together for the whole region and would be a help to them in combating the loneliness that affects so many missionary priests.

Father Hugo set about building such a rectory. The result was a 22-room structure built of clinker brick (brick that has been over-burned in the oven). It still stands as one of the most remarkable buildings in Mangum. In the years to come, two priests, and sometimes three, would live there and commute to the outlying mission parishes.

A great change came to Mangum and its missions in 1950, when Dominican priests from Chicago accepted Bishop McGuinness' invitation to live and work in southwest Oklahoma. For twelve years the Dominicans labored in the region. Their successor was Father Joseph Burger, whose first order of business was to build a new and larger church to replace the building of 1902.

Whereas in its early years the parish had been distinguished ethnically by Czech-speaking farm families, by the 1960's it was notable for its Hispanics. In 1965 there were 150 Anglo-Americans and 100 Hispanics at Sacred Heart.

✦ Father Willem Huffer had his picture taken with children from an Oklahoma mission parish, around 1940.

Wichita & Affiliated Tribes

August 6, 1901

BY 1895 it was apparent that land runs, though they seemed to put everyone on an equal footing, were quite vulnerable to cheating. Many people who claimed land honestly had to endure court battles with those who reached the claim later but could find witnesses to testify to their prior right. Cases involving conflicting claims dragged on for years through the 1890's, and there was no guarantee that a genuine claimant's right would be upheld in a given case.

When agreements were made with the tribes involved in the last great openings, therefore, it was decided that acreages would be assigned by lottery. On June 9, 1901, the Wichita and Caddo lands, west of the 98th Meridian between the South Canadian and the Washita Rivers, together with the lands belonging jointly to the Kiowas, Comanches, and Apaches, which lay to the south of the other reservations, were declared open. 170,000 persons registered for the lottery, with 13,000 quarter-sections available for settlement. The lottery commenced at El Reno and Kingfisher on August 6, with one thousand names drawn each day from three large revolving drums. The proposed boundaries of the reservation were part of an 1869 bill that was never ratified by Congress. The Wichita and Caddo lands today are generally equivalent to Caddo County north of the Washita, and those parts of Blaine, Canadian, and Grady Counties south of the South Canadian.

July-Aug. 1901

•Anadarko

BINGER
Our Lady of the Rosary

Caddoes. It appears that the founder of the Binger mission was Father Aloysius Hitta, O.S.B. Father Aloysius was assistant to Father Isidore Ricklin, O.S.B., director of St. Patrick's Mission at Anadarko, until the latter's death in 1921; then he was himself director until the school closed in 1966.

Since St. Patrick's educated numerous Caddo children, along with Kiowas, Comanches, and Apaches, it is reasonable to suppose that Father Aloysius had a strong interest in providing a church for them in their hometown. In 1932 Immaculate Conception church opened at Cyril, also in Caddo County; it was designated for use by Mexicans living in the area. For some years the director of St. Patrick's cared for both Binger and Cyril, but by 1950 Binger was under the care of the pastor at Hinton, while Cyril was attached to Apache. In 1956 a new church was built at Binger, dedicated to Our Lady of the Holy Rosary. Currently Binger is served from Anadarko.

Binger is in Caddo County, twelve miles south of Hinton. Its church was originally founded as St. Margaret Mary's in 1931 to serve Caddo Catholics, for Binger is the center for most of the remaining

HINTON
Sacred Heart

The first Catholics in the Hinton area entered the country when the Wichita-Caddo lands opened in June 1901. The first Mass in Hinton was offered on August 26, 1904, by Father John van den Hende, pastor of Hydro. Father Casper Douenburg became the first resident pastor of Hinton in 1905; he built Sacred Heart Church, which Bishop Meerschaert blessed on February 15, 1906.

Hinton continued as a parish and as a center for missionary activity until 1969, when it became a mission of Weatherford. During the 1960's, it is said, parishioner numbers dwindled to such a low that there were not enough men to serve as pallbearers. During the 1970's, however, there was a slow increase, and beginning in the 1980's there was an influx of Mexican migrant farm workers. Today the parish, served from Weatherford, is about 50 percent Hispanic.

Comanche, Kiowa and Apache Lands

June 9 - August 6, 1901

A<small>T</small> the same time that the Wichita and Caddo lands were opened, the much larger tract that had been assigned to the Comanches, the Kiowas, and the Apaches by treaties of 1865 and 1867 was also opened to white settlement. In this "new country" the government located and surveyed a few principal towns. Once the tribal members had received their allotments, the acreages and town lots were sold to the highest bidder on designated dates. This took place at Lawton and Anadarko in August 1901. A total of 2,968,893 acres, (18,555 quarter sections) were available for assignment. The region, except for a southern portion known as the Big Pasture, consisted of everything in the present State of Oklahoma lying south of the Washita River (and the Cheyenne Arapaho reservation) and extending westward from the 98th Meridian to Old Greer County and the western boundary of the state. Modern jurisdictions included are the south part of Caddo County, the far western portions of Grady, Stephens, and Jefferson Counties, and all of Kiowa, Comanche, Tillman, and Cotton Counties.

July-Aug. 1901

•Lawton

❖ St. Patrick Church.

ANADARKO

St. Patrick

In 1871 the government had established the federal Indian Agency at Anadarko, and the tribes offered quarter-section parcels to agents for the Baptists, Methodists, and Presbyterians. In 1885 a similar offer was made to the Benedictines at Sacred Heart. As with the other missions, it was near the Anadarko Agency that Father Isidore built the Catholics' school. Initial funding came from the monastery, but Bishop Meerschaert soon interested himself in the project and undertook to raise funds for it. This took him to Pennsylvania and the convent of St. Katharine Drexel, to whom he presented a letter of introduction from Archbishop Patrick John Ryan of Philadelphia. The note read, "Dear Mother Katharine, please do what you can for this poor missionary bishop, for all he has to his name is a mere shirt." Archbishop Ryan was rewarded for this pun on the bishop's name by having the Anadarko school named in honor of his patron saint.

O N the same day that Theophile Meerschaert was ordained in Mississippi as Oklahoma's first bishop, a young Benedictine monk set out from Sacred Heart Mission, Indian Territory, on his way to start St. Patrick's mission school for Caddo, Wichita, Comanche, Kiowa, Delaware, Kiowa-Apache, and Ft. Still Apache Indians. The date was September 8, 1891, and the young monk was Father Isidore Ricklin, O.S.B. Before any of the western Indian lands had yet been opened to white settlement, this intrepid priest laid the groundwork for a mission establishment whose size and scope would come to rival that of Sacred Heart itself.

He began by visiting the Plains Indians' camps and villages, accepting their hospitality and explaining what he hoped to do. His rapport with the Kiowas was infectious, and he soon won the trust he needed. He was not the only missionary to the seven tribes; several other denominations worked to build mission schools, too, but Father Isidore's was the only one that lasted—right up to 1966, in fact.

Chief Quanah Parker had included Father Isidore on the Comanche roll, and he was given an allotment. Upon the opening of the reservation lands in 1901, a lottery and sale of town lots was held at Anadarko on August 14. Father Isidore paid $463.00 for three town lots. The money was contributed by the prospective settlers and business people, among whom he had discovered a number of Catholics. Work on the parish church was begun in November. Carpenters were in great demand, and building material could not be shipped in fast enough to supply the needs. Yet the building was completed sufficiently by January 1902 that he could celebrate Mass in it, five months after the birth of the town.

On June 10 of the same year, Bishop Theophile Meerschaert dedicated the church to the Holy Family. The completed building cost $1,200 and was paid for with contributions from people of all classes, professions and religions.

In 1967 St. Patrick Church was constructed on the grounds of St. Patrick Indian Mission under Father James Murphy, O.S.B. Holy Family and St. Patrick Churches were taken care of by the Benediction monks until 1974 when Father Mike Chapman, the first diocesan priest, was assigned to Anadarko.

❖ Left: Holy Family Church.
❖ Above: St. Patrick Indian mission school.

APACHE
Mother of Sorrows

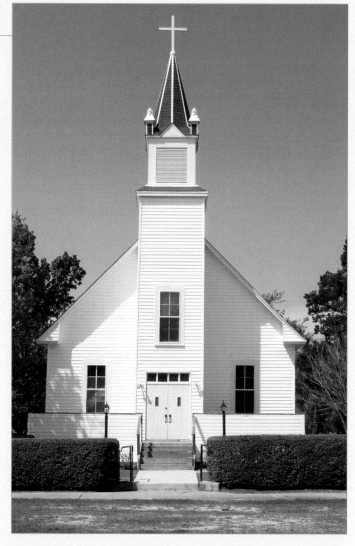

URBAN de Hasque was a young Belgian priest, newly ordained and less than one year in the United States, when he wrote the following account: "My first visit to Apache occurred on October 9, 1901. I drove to it with one of Father Isidore [Ricklin's] teams on the occasion of a brief stay at St. Patrick's Mission of Anadarko. The following month I was appointed pastor of Chickasha with jurisdiction over the major part of the 'new country,' the Comanche-Kiowa-Caddo reservations opened for settlement during the summer of that year. Apache was about four months old, when I held there the first service on November 27 in George Rose's building.

"After that first Mass I returned regularly for the monthly service on the fourth Saturday. With the completion of the Herber Hotel, services were held there. Among the first residents were a number of families of German and Luxemburg descent whom I had known in Okarche... The congregation was rapidly organized. A committee secured options on vacant lots on which to build a church. Bishop Meerschaert came in person on April 9, 1902, to consider the real estate propositions, but the one he favored was not to be the one adopted by the committee. On May 24, after services in the Herber Hotel, I announced that henceforth Father Willy Huffer, recently appointed pastor of Lawton [and Father de Hasque's seminary classmate in Belgium], would look after the spiritual interests of the congregation of Apache.

"Sometime during the following two years the committee bought two sloping lots on which they built the church. As a number of people did not like the location, the contributions did not come in as promptly and as generously as the trustees had expected, with the result that when the structure was completed and ready for use, there remained a number of unpaid bills. The debt had not been settled in full in the summer of 1904, when during the temporary absence in Europe of Father Huffer, I celebrated Mass in the church on the first Sundays of July, August, September and October. There was then question of moving the building to a more spacious location on which eventually a rectory and perhaps a parochial school might be erected. This was done after Christmas 1905.

"The church stood on its new location, where it stands today, when I accompanied Bishop Meerschaert from Sterling to Apache and assisted him in the dedication of the building to Our Lady of the Seven Dolors on March 30, 1906, and in the Confirmation rite of a class of twenty-two children and adults. To the east of the church a rectory was built by Father [Frederick] Van der Aa, the first resident priest, who occupied it from 1907 to 1925. Plans for a parochial school have yet to be drawn." At present Apache is a mission of Elgin.

✦ Father Urban de Hasque.

CARNEGIE
St. Richard

CARNEGIE is in Caddo County, about eighteen miles west of Anadarko. On May 29, 1902, the first Mass was celebrated in the dugout home of Charles Shuman, about five miles north of Carnegie. Afterwards services were conducted occasionally either in public halls or private homes by the priest from Chickasha, Anadarko or Hobart. With the help of Catholic Extension, a building 16 by 30 feet was completed, in which the first Mass was offered on March 14, 1905. It was named in honor of Our Lady of Victory, possibly with reference to the shrine church of Notre Dame des Victoires in Paris, which was a favorite of Bishop Meerschaert.

On April 20, 1920, the second church building, located across the Rock Island tracks on Broadway, was acquired. It was remodeled, finished inside, and a steeple was added to the front. This chapel, too, was named Our Lady of Victory, and the Extension Society helped with it as well.

Bishop Kelley, before he came to Oklahoma in 1924, had been the founder and first president of the Extension Society. He brought with him as his secretary a priest who had served in a similar capacity at Extension's office in Chicago. This was Father Richard R. St. John, a native, like Kelley himself, of Prince Edward Island, Canada. Father St. John worked in Oklahoma for about four years, then he returned to Chicago to resume his work at Extension. At the time of his death in 1951 he was vice-president of Catholic Extension.

Wishing to build a church in his memory, the Extension Society chose to build it at Carnegie, under the title of St. Richard. The president of Extension, Archbishop William D. O'Brien, presided at the dedication on March 13, 1955.

ELGIN
St. Ann

schedule, until 1941, when it was finally raised to the status of a mission.

World War II, and the restrictions on building materials, delayed plans for a new church, but construction started in 1946, with much of the work done by the parishioners. It was completed in 1948, and Bishop McGuinness named it St. Ann. The old church served as the parish hall until 1967, when a new hall was built that included a small apartment for a priest.

ELGIN is eight miles west of Sterling and roughly eighteen miles northeast of Lawton. The first church, St. Anthony's, was located in a former schoolhouse that the congregation purchased some time between 1910 and 1914. Before that, Father William Lamb came from Lawton for Mass on weekdays. Elgin was a chapel of convenience, a place where local funerals and weddings could be celebrated, but without a regular Mass

In 1997, a rectory was built and the pastor moved from Sterling to Elgin. Thus the chapel from 1910 became a full-fledged parish in 1997. New classrooms were built for the religious education program in 2004.

FREDERICK
St. Helen

MASS was first offered in Frederick, seat of Tillman County, in 1902. The celebrant was Father Willem Huffer of Lawton. The first church, St. Francis of Assisi, opened in 1915, with Father John van Gastel of Hobart as construction supervisor. Father Joseph Kolb was assigned to reside in Frederick in 1957. Bishop Reed purchased property for a new church, which was built with much volunteer labor and a $10,000 grant from the Extension Society. At the request of an Extension donor, the church was named St. Helen's. Father Kolb offered the first Mass in the new church on May 28, 1961.

From the early 1960's to the late 1970's, the parish was served, first, by two Extension Lay Volunteers, then by Benedictine Sisters, and finally by Carmelite Sisters. They were all involved in home visitation and catechetical work.

In 1989 ground was broken for a new addition with a hall, a kitchen, and three classrooms. The cost was $116,000.00, made possible through the Extension Society, the archdiocese, ten archdiocesan parishes, and the contributions of parishioners. The parish now has about a hundred families, a large percentage of them Hispanic.

HOBART
Ss. Peter and Paul

THE Hobart parish may have been the farthest-flung mission served by the wide-ranging Jesuit missionary, Father Paul Ponziglione. Stationed in southeastern Kansas, he traveled by horse and buggy throughout Oklahoma in the 1870's. He made his first visit to the Kiowa country in 1875. After 1891, Father Isidore Ricklin or one of his Benedictine confreres would come from Anadarko to the Hobart area; and beginning in 1896, Father Zenon Steber visited the place from his headquarters at Corn in Washita County.

Hobart itself was surveyed as a townsite in 1901, in preparation for the opening in June, and town lots were sold to the highest bidder. On August 14 Captain Hill, acting on behalf of Father Isidore, bought three town lots for a church, and the priests offered the first Mass in town at the residence—quite possibly a tent-

of the Sherman family. In 1903 Father Willem Huffer began organizing the parish, promising to celebrate Mass on the third Sunday of every month. The parishioners were very poor, but they were determined to have a church. They managed to buy a frame building that had already served as a post office. By January 1904 it was ready for Mass.

A year later Bishop Meerschaert came to Hobart; he dedicated the church to the honor of Saints Peter and Paul on January 17, 1905. The following October he appointed Father Henry Kickx, a Belgian priest recently ordained, as pastor of Hobart. Father Kickx said the first Mass as pastor on March 17th. Father Kickx built an eight-room rectory, paying for it with his own money. His five years at Hobart were creative and productive.

Hobart continued as a parish until 1927, when it became a mission of Mangum. During the pastorate of Father Bernard Loftus (1945-1950), however, a new church and rectory were built, and Father Loftus moved into the rectory. For six months in 1968, the parish was without a resident pastor because Father Herman Schafers died in an airplane crash near Enid. In recent years, Hobart and Mangum have shared a pastor.

LAWTON
Blessed Sacrament

1905 Lawton received its third pastor, the newly ordained Father William P. Lamb. He was responsible for building the parish school and staffing it. The Sisters of Divine Providence, of San Antonio, Texas, had begun opening schools in Oklahoma. Their first school was at Perry in 1901. Father Lamb persuaded the Sisters to begin a school on the Lawton frontier. He put up a four-room frame building, and the Sisters opened St. Mary's Academy on September 2, 1907. Seventy-five students enrolled that first year.

In 1924 the frame church was destroyed by fire. Believing the disaster was the work of the Ku Klux Klan—though it is not clear this was actually the case—the citizens of Lawton raised funds toward the building of a new brick church. Its steeple made the new Blessed Sacrament Church the tallest building in Lawton. Father Lamb, then completing twenty years in Lawton, said the first Mass at the end of 1925, just before his replacement arrived.

Father Lamb's pastorate was the prelude to two other lengthy terms of office. Father Charles Van Hulse served Blessed Sacrament from 1925 to 1935 before retiring and living at Lawton as pastor emeritus until his death in 1951. Monsignor Ben Hulshof was pastor from 1935 until his own death in 1961.

In the years that followed, many significant events occurred in the life of this parish. Particularly notable was the work done at Blessed Sacrament in the wake of the Vietnam War. Father Elmer Robnett became famous for his one-man effort to solve the refugee crisis, even housing several families at once in the rectory basement.

I N 1869 the U.S. Army opened a frontier post named Fort Sill. Its purpose was to keep the peace among the southern tribes, especially the Comanches, who were conducting raids from their villages in Texas. An Indian trading post, called the Red Store, opened in 1886 a short distance from the fort, and this became the basis for the new town of Lawton when it came into existence on August 6, 1901.

The first priest to visit the new town was Father Isidore Ricklin, O.S.B., in charge of St. Patrick's Mission School near the Anadarko Indian agency. In 1902 Father Urban de Hasque, from Chickasha, visited the town. He offered Mass once a month in a store room on "E" St., and in the home of Dr. Joseph Mullen and his wife, Mary. Mass was offered on the fourth Sunday of each month. Bishop Meerschaert traveled to Lawton in June 1902, and introduced his traveling companion, Father Zenon Steber, as the first resident pastor of Lawton.

❖ Blessed Sacrament School.

Lawton Catholics bought land on the corner of Seventh Street and what is now Gore Boulevard. Father Steber remained only a few months, being succeeded by Father Willem Huffer in November 1902. Father Huffer oversaw construction of a frame church and rectory on the new site. Bishop Meerschaert dedicated this church to the Blessed Sacrament on August 19, 1903.

The vast areas being opened and populated, and the small number of priests available to serve them, forced the bishop to move his priests like pawns on a busy chessboard. In October

❖ The Van Hulse brothers—Charles, Joseph, and Theophile—all missionaries in Oklahoma.

LAWTON
Holy Family

THE second parish in Lawton was begun in June 1959 when Father Paul Mollan, the first pastor, celebrated Mass at the Vaska Theatre. The parish was begun to serve families from nearby Ft. Sill, and it was dedicated to St. Barbara, patron saint of artillerymen. The first church and school were dedicated on her feast day, December 4, 1960. By 1978, though, St. Barbara's had outgrown its original location, and the entire property was sold to the Lawton public school system, with the stipulation that the parish could remain on it for a further two years. On June 19, 1979, ground was broken at 1010 Northwest 82nd Street, and on November 1 of that year St. Barbara's officially became Holy Family. In October 1980, Archbishop Charles Salatka formally dedicated a new church, rectory, and religious education classrooms. By 1993 the parish numbered over 1000 families, and a vision of a Family Life Center had begun to unfold. In the fall of 1996 this 19,000-square-foot building was dedicated by Archbishop Beltran.

RYAN
San Jose

ALTHOUGH much recent parish development in southern Oklahoma has been driven by the presence of Hispanic migrant workers, few parishes have been established especially for them. One of them is San Jose in Jefferson County, originally located in Sugden in 1974 and now at Ryan. At present the parish is attended by the pastor of Duncan.

TIPTON
Sacred Heart

FATHER Joseph Kolb offered the first Mass in Tipton, ten miles northwest of Frederick, during a vacation Bible school there in 1961. In subsequent years, Mass was offered on occasion in an office building, a United Methodist church, and a Pentecostal Holiness church. Finally Sacred Heart Church was built in 1972, and dedicated on April 19 of that year by Bishop John R. Quinn.

STERLING
Our Lady of Perpetual Help

THE first Mass in the Sterling area was offered on August 21, 1902, in the dugout home of Martin Ille. Father Urban de Hasque from Chickasha rode a mail hack, a horse-and-buggy conveyance, to reach Sterling for Mass on weekdays. Once the Lawton parish was established, Father Willem Huffer cared for Sterling and Apache. The first church was built in 1904; apparently it was never blessed, but it was named in honor of Our Lady of Perpetual Help. It was considerably improved during the pastorate of the first resident priest, Father Anthony Van der Grinten. It had been in use for nearly 25 years, when, on December 22, 1928, it was totally destroyed by fire.

In February 1929 the contract for building the second church was awarded to C. J. Cannovan of Rush Springs. The plans, drawn by A.P. Landoll of Lawton, called for a building 30 feet by 72, in Roman style, with a tower 56 feet high. It was dedicated by Monsignor Gustave Depreitere on October 8, 1929. Today the congregation includes parishioners who are fifth generation members of the Sterling parish. Our Lady of Perpetual Help observed its centennial with Archbishop Beltran on September 19, 2004.

WALTERS
St. Patrick

O VER the years, St. Patrick's in Walters has provided pastoral care to Catholics in Cotton County—including Randlett, Devol, Taylor, Cookietown, and Temple—as well as Empire City and Comanche in Stephens County, and Geronimo in Jefferson County. The first church was a frame building erected by Father Frederick Van der Aa of Apache, and dedicated to St. Luke on November 23, 1910. After Father Leo Claus became the resident pastor, he promoted construction of a new place of worship in 1927. It was an attractive building of brick and stucco in the Spanish mission style, 27 feet wide and 61 feet long. After forty years of service, this building was condemned as unsafe, and it was necessary to build a new church. The building committee raised $18,000 from parishioners and area businesses, and the Extension Society contributed another $10,000. Bishop Reed dedicated the new church to the honor of St. Patrick on October 20, 1968.

From 1920 to 1964, Walters had a resident pastor who also cared for the missions of Grandfield and Waurika. From 1964 to 1989, it was a mission with pastors coming variously from Lawton, Sterling, Duncan, or Marlow. It achieved independent status again in 1989, but recently it has once more been a mission under the care of the pastor of Frederick.

WAURIKA
St. Thomas Aquinas Chapel

from parishioners and town businessmen. Some sixty names and amounts are listed among the contributors. Bishop Meerschaert presided at the dedication on December 16, 1915. He noted in his diary that the church was "a nice brick church, a credit to the place."

A S early as 1904 Catholics in Waurika were assembling for worship. In 1907, when Waurika was named the seat of Jefferson County (replacing Ryan), Catholics met in the courthouse there. The present church was built in 1915, with the help of $500.00 from the Extension Society and contributions

The church was originally dedicated to St. Mary. The use of St. Thomas Aquinas as titular first appears in the *Official Catholic Directory* in 1932. A vestibule was added later, and the sacristy enlarged. In 1995 a statue of St. Thomas Aquinas, imported from Spain, was donated by the Stuart family.

The Big Pasture

September 19, 1906

ALTHOUGH the greater part of the Kiowa, Comanche, and Apache lands were allotted in 1892 and finally opened in 1901, a 480,000-acre portion of the reservation, fronting on the Red River, had earlier been leased to Texas cattlemen to provide revenue for the tribes. Ending these leases caused a five-year delay in opening this final tract in western Oklahoma to non-Indian settlement.

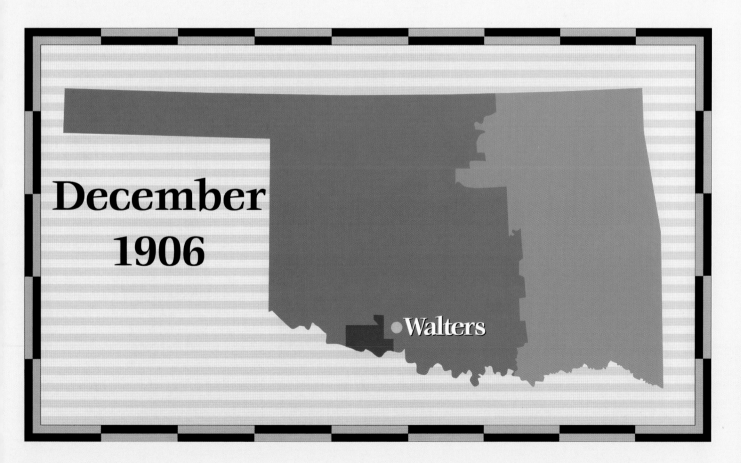

December 1906

Walters

GRANDFIELD
Our Lady of Perpetual Help

TOWARD the end of 1907, Father Anthony Vander Grinten, assistant pastor at Lawton, offered Mass for the first time at Chattanooga in the newly-opened Big Pasture area. In 1908 he occasionally offered Mass at Eschita, some fourteen miles south. In 1909 Eschita changed its name to Grandfield. Priests from Lawton continued to say Mass in homes and in Grandfield's Masonic Hall, but an oil boom in 1916 made it possible to buy lots and build a church, which was ready for Christmas Midnight Mass that year. There were then thirteen Catholic families in the area. Bishop Meerschaert dedicated the church on April 24, 1918, and confirmed eighteen persons.

The same church has continued in use to this day with only minor modifications. In the 1920's Grandfield was a mission of Walters until the Frederick parish was begun in 1957.

It was then served by Frederick pastors until 1989, when it was once more attached to Walters. In the past few years, however, it has again become a mission of Frederick.

Chickasaw Nation

THIS book is organized on the premise that the Church followed the pioneers who settled on the plains of Oklahoma in the period from the first Land Run in 1889 to statehood in 1907. This is generally true, but it ignores an already existing part of the state, the Indian Territory.

The term "Indian Territory" was first used in 1834 with reference to setting aside the entire area between the Rocky Mountains and the Mississippi River as a permanent homeland for the tribes being relocated from east of the great river by the press of American expansion. The proposed legislation was not enacted, but Indian Territory became the name for any part of the United States that was not a state or a territory—in other words, for most of the Louisiana Purchase. In 1834 this still encompassed a very great stretch of land, but in succeeding years, as new territories and states were carved from it, it steadily shrank, until by 1870 it was practically coterminous with modern Oklahoma.

Andrew Jackson of Tennessee was elected president in 1824 on a platform that promised to rid the southern states of Native Americans who still laid claim to land desirable for plantations. Treaties were made in 1825 that induced five major tribes in the American Southeast to relinquish their claims and move west of the Mississippi.

These were the so-called Civilized Tribes—the Cherokees, Creeks, Choctaws, Chickasaws, and Seminoles—who had lived peaceably with whites for over two centuries and had adopted many of their ideas about government and education. The land they received in 1825 amounted to most of Oklahoma. In 1866, however, since the tribes' sympathies had been with the Confederacy during the recent Civil War, they were made to suffer the loss of the western parts of their Oklahoma lands, which were then used for relocating the Plains tribes that had survived the Indian wars of the 1870's.

Land belonging to the Chickasaws and the Seminoles now lies within the Archdiocese of Oklahoma City. The Chickasaw Nation extends south from the Canadian River, and east from the 98th Meridian to about modern Lake Texoma. Although still claimed by the Chickasaws in some respects, it was absorbed into the new State of Oklahoma on November 16, 1907. It includes the following counties: McClain, Garvin, Murray, Carter, Love, Pontotoc, Johnston, and Marshall, with the greater parts of Stephens and Jefferson Counties.

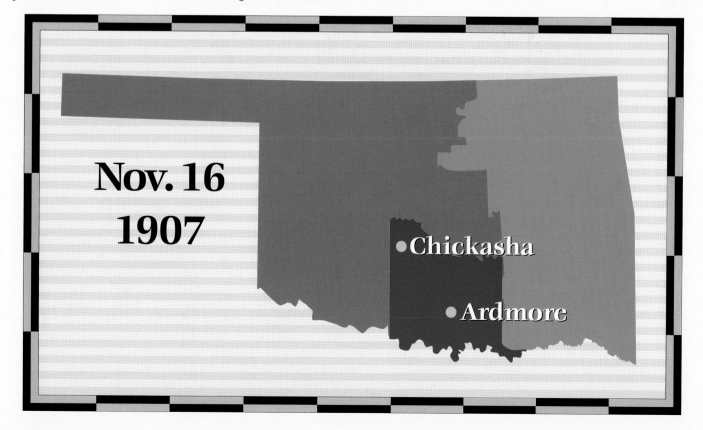

Nov. 16 1907

●Chickasha

●Ardmore

ADA
St. Joseph

succeeded in replacing the temporary chapel with a stone-faced block church, which he inaugurated on Easter of that year with a mission for non-Catholics. The new church was named for St. Joseph.

Beginning around 1927, the Benedictine monks of St. Gregory's Abbey in Shawnee became responsible for the pastorate at Ada. By 1935 there were a hundred families in the parish, and the monks had built a six-room rectory beside the church. 1954 saw construction of a school with four classrooms and a gymnasium auditorium, a convent for the Benedictine Sisters from Fort Smith, Arkansas, who would teach there, and a new rectory. The new St. Joseph Church was opened on Christmas Eve 1962. Built under the supervision of Father John Bloms, O.S.B., it features a 145-foot-high, free-standing bell tower and a vast stained glass window that forms the façade of the building. Bishop Reed conducted the dedication on May 7, 1963.

The Benedictines relinquished the Ada pastorate in 1975, after almost fifty years of service. At the same time, the school closed. The parish adjusted to these changes, and the years since have seen a series of renovations and improvements to the existing facilities.

ADA, the county seat of Pontotoc County, was named in 1891 for the daughter of the town's first postmaster. The first Mass was offered by Father Francis Hall of Ardmore in 1902 at the home of Jerry Cragin, but such ministry that followed was limited and sporadic.

Father Theophile Caudron, a tiny dynamo of a man, was ordained in 1907 and became pastor of Henryetta in 1912. He was one of Bishop Meerschaert's Belgian recruits, and it seemed as nothing to him to travel 65 miles by rail to Ada to support the tiny Catholic community there. When he promoted the erection in Ada of a place of worship, around 1916, he had to be satisfied with what he described as "an old cold drink stand," a small business building which was remodeled to serve as the first, quite unpretentious, Catholic church in the town. By the following year, however, with the growth of Ada and of the congregation, he

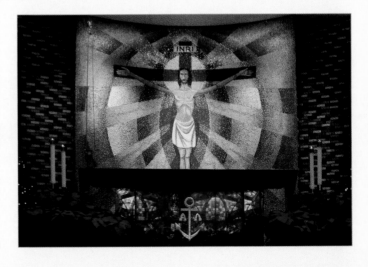

ARDMORE ◇ *St. Mary*

SOUTH of Purcell, the towns along the Santa Fe line are named in sequence for stops on the Philadelphia Main Line, so that Ardmore received its name from a corresponding city in Pennsylvania. Monks from Sacred Heart visited the Indian Territory town as early as 1889, but a church was not built until 1898. In the meantime a succession of priests from Purcell and Norman offered Mass in private homes.

Dick McLish, chairman of the Chickasaw tribe, donated the land for the church and school at Ardmore. Construction funds were provided by Father Raphael Ghewey and his sister Mathilda, Belgian friends of Bishop Meerschaert. They made a donation of $1,800. With this sum a church was built in 1897 and furnished with a main altar, pews, and vestments. The church was dedicated to Our Lady of Prompt Succor (also known as Our Lady of Perpetual Help), because in December 1895 the bishop had been stricken with Bright's Disease, and he credited his almost miraculous recovery to prayers offered at the shrine of Our Lady of Prompt Succor at the Ursuline Convent in New Orleans.

The church was dedicated on August 28, 1898. That same day the bishop also dedicated in Ardmore the new St. Agnes Academy for girls, served by the Sisters of Mercy and built with the financial assistance of St. Katharine Drexel.

With the completion of the church and the erection of a two-room rectory the congregation received its first resident pastor, Father Francis Hall. He remained in charge for five years. He was followed by Father Peter Wilwerding

(1902-1905), and then by Father James J. Wallrapp, who would serve until 1929. At first the parish consisted of everything that is now Carter, Love, Murray, Jefferson, Bryan, Marshall, Garvin, Johnston, and part of Pontotoc Counties—or, as the *Official Catholic Directory* put it, "from Davis to the Texas line." In 1908 additional missions were established and assigned to other parishes.

The new church was severely tested in its early years. In 1906 and again in the spring of 1915, violent storms nearly destroyed the building. Then, on September 27, 1915, a gasoline-filled tank car in the nearby rail yard exploded, blowing out several stained glass windows. This famous disaster, which killed 51 persons, wounded another 150, and caused nearly a million dollars in property damage, became the catalyst for greatly improved safety procedures for the transport of volatile substances.

In 1950, Father Alexander Andrews, a British missionary who had worked in Burma as a translator with the 45th Infantry Division during World War II, arrived in Oklahoma seeking a respite for his health. The parish had been raising funds for a new church, and Father Andrews oversaw its construction. On December 8, 1951, Bishop McGuinness dedicated the new building under the title of St. Mary, Our Lady of the Rosary. A new school soon followed, which continued until 1966.

Father Andrews also was responsible for a new mission church in Sulphur, St. Francis, in 1954. He died of cancer the day it was dedicated. (His nephew, Father Bernard Jewitt, was ordained to the priesthood five years later.) A second mission, St. Cecilia's in Healdton, was dedicated in 1955. Ardmore's third mission, Good Shepherd in Marietta, was opened in 1993, making Love County the last one in the archdiocese to host a Catholic congregation.

In 2002 Archbishop Beltran was not able to continue sending a pastor to Sulphur, Madill, and Tishomingo.

Sulphur became an independent parish, but in 2002 it was transferred to the pastoral care of Ada, and its missions of Madill and Tishomingo were attached to the Ardmore parish.

Chickasha
Holy Name

THE Rock Island railroad, building south from Kansas, reached the site of Chickasha in April 1892. At first there were no settlers except for the railroaders themselves. When they petitioned the U.S. Post Office to name their town Chickasaw, a clerk there misspelled the name as Chickasha, and nothing was ever done about it. Among the railroad workers were a number of mostly Irish Catholics. The pastor of El Reno came on a weekday once a month to say Mass in one or another Catholic homes. In 1895 the bishop appointed Father Joseph Van Hulse as the first resident pastor. There was a church in the parish, but it was at Minco, twenty miles north. The next year Father Francis Hall, newly ordained, became the second pastor, but even though the area was by then expanding rapidly, the project of building a church did not catch fire.

Father Hall had one notable experience while at Chickasha. He happened to be traveling on a train near Pocasset, north of Chickasha, when the outlaws Al and Frank Jennings boarded and proceeded to rob the passengers. (The gang was later captured and tried in Muskogee.)

The Chickasha parish was temporarily entrusted to Father Isidore Ricklin, O.S.B., director of St. Patrick's Mission at Anadarko, and it was he that finally succeeded in erecting a small frame church early in 1898. It was dedicated to the Holy Name of Jesus by Bishop Meerschaert on May 15, 1898. In 1899 the Franciscan Sisters of Philadelphia, with the help of St. Katharine Drexel, opened St. Joseph's Academy; it would operate for 69 years. Under the pastorate of Father Urban de Hasque (1901-12) the church was moved four hundred feet to the northeast corner of Block 53, the "school block," to which he had secured clear title. He enlarged it to double its seating capacity, and it was rededicated on May 7, 1908. While Father Frank Van Wees was pastor, a new brick church was built; it was dedicated on May 2, 1926.

The parish in Chickasha may be better known for its parishioners than for its buildings. Besides distinguishing themselves professionally, a number of them have become priests and sisters. Three members of the Ross family have been ordained to the priesthood.

DUNCAN
Assumption

FATHER Urban de Hasque of Chickasha offered Mass in Duncan, Rush Springs, and Marlow on a regular basis from 1901 until 1912. His first Mass in Duncan was on December 12, 1902. It was in the home of Mr. and Mrs. John Weaver on Beech Avenue. Later, Mr. and Mrs. John O'Neill moved to town from a ranch near Velma, and they kept a room they called the chapel room. The first Sunday Mass was offered there in October 1905. Mr. and Mrs. J.D. Wade, along with Dr. Kuery, gave new impetus to the parish's growth; Mr. Wade was a banker. John O'Neill began the campaign for a new church, promising $500.00 upon completion of the structure. Father de Hasque said the first Mass on January 1, 1909, before a congregation of twenty-one Catholics. Six weeks later, Father Michael McManus was appointed the first resident pastor. Within two months he was able to move into a new four-room rectory.

April 20, 1909, was the dedication day for the new church, which was named in honor of the Assumption of the Blessed Virgin Mary.

In the early 1920's there was an oil boom in Duncan, but it was short-lived. A new school, named for St. Joan of Arc (she was newly canonized), opened in 1921. The school closed in 1926, only to reopen 20 years later as Sacred Heart School. In 1960, on Easter Sunday, the parish offered Mass in Duncan's new Assumption Church.

In 1938 Adolf Hitler annexed Austria as part of his vision of a greater Germany. The chancellor of Austria then was Kurt Schussnig, a Catholic, and his confessor in Vienna was Father George Fangauer, of the Oblates of St. Francis de Sales. When Schussnig was arrested by the Gestapo, Father Fangauer had to flee. A year later he arrived in Oklahoma at the invitation of Bishop Kelley and was assigned as pastor of Duncan. From 1939 until 1999, Father Fangauer and other members of his order served Duncan and its missions of Marlow and Rush Springs.

More recently, the Duncan pastor has also had charge of San Jose church in Ryan, and other missions in the southwest area of the state as well.

HEALDTON
St. Cecilia

HEALDTON, in western Carter County, was the scene of considerable oil development during the 1950's. This led to St. Cecilia's being built in 1955; the work was directed by Father Ramon Carlin, pastor of Ardmore. Still a mission of Ardmore, St. Cecilia's features original works by Oklahoma-born artist Father John Walch.

LINDSAY
St. Peter

place for the Benedictine missionaries traveling to Anadarko and Ft. Sill.

In 1902 the Santa Fe and Rock Island railroads agreed to create a town on the north bank of the Washita, across the river from Erin Springs. It was named Lindsay, after Frank Murray's son-in-law, Lewis Lindsay, who gave part of his land for the townsite. Father Urban de Hasque, pastor at Chickasha, came regularly to say Mass at Lindsay. In 1903 he obtained land for a church, but the project suffered delays, and it was only when Father de Hasque was about to be transferred from Chickasha that he was able to persuade the Lindsay Catholics to get started on their church. The Extension Society provided a grant of $500.00, with the stipulation that the church be named for St. Louis of France, in accord with a donor's wish. Others made smaller contributions, and the church was built for $1600.00. Father de Hasque offered the first Mass on September 12, 1912, and it was dedicated on May 18, 1913.

Lindsay was cared for by the pastor of Duncan until 1917; then it was a mission of the monks of St. Gregory's Abbey, notably Father Blaise Hartichabalet, O.S.B., who served it monthly from 1924 until his death in 1949. That same year, a parish was established at Pauls Valley with a resident pastor, and Lindsay became its mission. With that impetus, planning began for a new church, and St. Peter's was dedicated on March 13, 1955, with a generous donation from Monsignor Matthew Canning, a Chicago pastor. The altar, built of mahogany, was donated by the Lindsay family.

A LTHOUGH no church was ever built there, the town of Erin Springs is pivotal to the history of Catholicism in Garvin County. The town began as a relay station on the Washita River, where stagecoach drivers on their way to Ft. Sill could change horses. A large tree stood nearby, and the place was first called Edgewood, then Elm Springs. In 1871 an Irish immigrant, Frank Murray, and his Irish-Choctaw wife, Alzira, settled in the tiny settlement of Pauls Valley. Shortly thereafter, they moved twenty-five miles west to the site of Elm Springs. They were the first settlers in the place. Because of reciprocity between the Choctaws and Chickasaws, Frank Murray, as an intermarried Choctaw citizen, could lay claim to unlimited acreage in the Chickasaw Nation. Eventually he would farm and ranch some 20,000 acres; a single cornfield encompassed 8,000 acres. The couple built a large and impressive mansion, which still stands. Over time, Elm Springs became Erin Springs, named for Frank Murray's sister.

Frank Murray was a staunch Catholic, and Alzira was baptized in 1885. Their home became a welcome stopping

MADILL
Holy Cross

A LTHOUGH Mass had been offered in Madill as early as 1914, there was no continuity in the ministry there, and it was not until 1949 that a church was actually constructed. After Mr. and Mrs. Max Jones donated a lot on the corner of First and Francis for a new church, Bishop McGuinness bought an adjacent duplex for a rectory and chapel in May 1948. Father Warren Kerns, pastor of Durant, had charge of the work of converting this structure for parish use. Bishop McGuinness blessed the church and rectory on January 29, 1950. The present Holy Cross church was built in 1957 and renovated in accordance with the reforms of Vatican II in 1967. A

parish hall addition was built in 1981 and a classroom wing in 1991. A Mass in Spanish was added to the schedule to accommodate increasing numbers of Hispanic parishioners.

Marlow
Immaculate Conception

THE first priest to celebrate Mass occasionally in Marlow was Father Elias Fink, O.S.B. As assistant to Father Isidore Ricklin at St. Patrick's Mission, Anadarko, he was stationed at Chickasha in 1900. Father Urban de Hasque, who became pastor of Chickasha in November 1901, first undertook to conduct a service once a month on a weekday; then, on a Sunday every two months (alternating with Rush Springs); and finally, from October 1903, regularly on the second Sunday of each month.

Before a church was built the weekday services were always held in the residence of Mr. Tom Wade, then cashier of the National Bank of Marlow. It was principally through his influence that the cherished project of Father Urban to build a Catholic church in Marlow was carried out. Four vacant lots, property belonging to Tom Wade, were selected for the church, and on December 1, 1902, they were deeded to Bishop Meerschaert for a consideration of one dollar. When sufficient funds, collected principally from the Wade brothers, were available, construction of a frame building measuring 30 by 35 feet, with a sacristy in the rear, was undertaken in the summer of 1904. Bishop Meerschaert came to dedicate it to the Immaculate Conception, on November 22, 1904, during the fiftieth anniversary year of the proclamation of this dogma of faith.

Just six months later, however, a windstorm moved the structure about 20 feet off its foundation, without wrecking it, but leaving it standing in an unlevel position. The dismay of the congregation and the pastor was intensified when it was learned that Mr. Tom Wade, who was also an insurance agent, had failed to insure the building against damage from high winds. But Tom never blinked. When, two days later, the pastor arrived from Chickasha to appraise the situation, he learned Wade had already entered into an agreement with a contractor to replace the building on a lower foundation in the best possible condition. It was done without delay and without cost to the congregation. Tom Wade paid the bill in full.

In 1912 the church of Marlow was placed in the pastoral charge of the priest residing at Duncan, ten miles south. In 1996 the congregation built a new fellowship hall, but the only site available on which to construct a new church was that of the 1904 church. In 1997 the venerable structure was again moved off its foundation and transported through the town to a new home in the city park, where it now serves as an interdenominational chapel. Then the parish built its new church, which Archbishop Beltran dedicated on November 7, 1999.

MARIETTA
Good Shepherd

WHEN Father Ernest Flusche was pastor of Ardmore, he became convinced of the need to provide more services for the Spanish-speaking migrant workers of the area. Many of them were gathered in Love County, south of Ardmore, and this was one of two Oklahoma counties that had never had a church of its own. A first attempt at a Hispanic parish was made in November 1993 at Thackerville, in the extreme southern part of the county, but it soon developed that Marietta, the county seat, would provide a more feasible location.

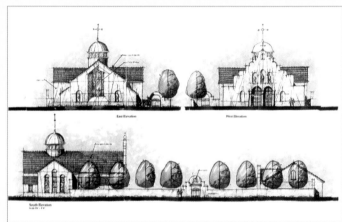

Fundraising is now underway for a new church, planned for a two-acre site in Marietta.

PAULS VALLEY
St. Catherine of Siena

PAULS VALLEY, named for early settler Smith Paul, developed on the Chickasaw plains around 1870. Nearly eighty years would pass before the town, by now in Garvin County, became the site of a Catholic church.

In 1949, Bishop McGuinness made a trip to Europe, where he sought priestly personnel from Ireland and among the displaced priests of Poland. He also met Father Joseph Duffy, a young, energetic priest from Salford, England, who was interested in coming to Oklahoma. Immediately upon his arrival he was assigned as the first pastor of Pauls Valley. He offered his first Mass at the Stuffelbean Funeral Home on October 2, 1949. By the late spring of 1950 he

had managed to build a church and a rectory. Funds for the project came from Katherine Price of Philadelphia, a philanthropist and a friend of Bishop McGuinness. In her honor the church was dedicated to St. Catherine of Siena.

PURCELL
Our Lady of Victory

WHEN the Land Run of 1889 occurred, there had already been a Catholic church in Purcell for three years. Father Frank Rouquier, a mysterious figure, appeared in the Indian Territory in 1886, was assigned to Purcell, and built a church on the corner of Second and Adams. Then he disappeared, only to surface again on the Quapaw reservation for a brief time in 1890, before vanishing for good. A search of the Catholic directories for the United States and Canada over a 30-year period finds him nowhere but at Purcell and Quapaw.

In September 1888 St. Elizabeth's Mission School for Chickasaw Girls opened at Purcell, being a project of Miss Catharine Drexel, who was soon to become Mother Mary Katharine Drexel, one of the American church's greatest benefactors, the foundress of a religious community, and a canonized saint. St. Elizabeth's, named for the patron of Catharine Drexel's sister, operated in Purcell until 1948. On the day of the Land Run, the school, sited on top of Red Hill, provided the perfect vantage point for observers of the great events in the Canadian River valley below.

The day before the Run, which was Easter Sunday, Father Ignatius Jean, O.S.B., the apostolic prefect of the Indian Territory, preached to a large crowd that had gathered in anticipation of crossing into "the land flowing with milk and honey." His sermon, whose text has been preserved, encouraged the prospective settlers to raise their children as Christians, to respect the laws of marriage, and to honor the rights of the Native Americans already at home in the territory.

Purcell was the center of all this activity because it was a station on the Santa Fe railroad, and it was located just south of the Unassigned Lands, that would soon become Oklahoma Territory. The railroad was built through Oklahoma in 1886 and 1887, and the town was named for a vice-president of the Santa Fe.

In September 1891 Bishop Meerschaert was ordained at St. Mary's Cathedral in Natchez, Mississippi, having been named apostolic vicar of the Indian Territory. He then set out for his new charge, arriving in Purcell on September 18. He said Mass in the chapel of St. Elizabeth's school, his first Mass in the Territory, before proceeding to Guthrie and a civic reception there the next day.

Because the small church was located some distance from the school atop Red Hill, it made sense to erect another, larger, church next to the school. This was done in 1892. The new bishop blessed the cornerstone of Our Lady of Victory on March 23 of that year, and dedicated the finished building on August 21. The 1886 church was moved to the new site and used as a parish school for boys.

The Canadian River flows directly south as it passes Purcell. Separated by the river from Purcell, and lying to its east, is the town of Lexington. St. John the Baptist church opened there in 1890 and served for over a century, until the Lexington parish was closed in 1999.

The third, and present, Purcell church was dedicated in 1952. Of Romanesque design, it contained windows and altars from Our Lady's Cathedral in Oklahoma City, which had recently been remodeled. On April 2, 2000, Archbishop Beltran dedicated a fine new parish hall at Our Lady of Victory.

RUSH SPRINGS
St. Francis of Assisi

for Rush Springs was the nearest stop on the railroad for northbound travelers from the fort. As early as 1894 the bishop presided at a discussion in the Huntley home about prospects for a church in Rush Springs.

It was not until 1918, however, that a church was actually built there. Father Emil Ghyssaert, pastor of Duncan, offered the first Mass in August of that year, and the bishop returned for the dedication of St. Francis of Assisi Church on March 30, 1919. The Extension Society contributed toward the construction, and the church was named St. Francis to commemorate Extension's president, Father Francis Kelley, who became Oklahoma's bishop five years later.

MASS was offered as early as 1880 in this region by the first apostolic prefect of the Indian Territory, Dom Isidore Robot, O.S.B. In the years that followed priests celebrated the Eucharist occasionally in the homes of Frank Murray, S.M. Huntley, or John Coyle. Bishop Meerschaert, on his way to and from Ft. Sill, was a not infrequent visitor,

TISHOMINGO ◇ St. Anthony

TISHOMINGO, in Johnston County, is the original capital of the Chickasaw Nation. In his diary, Bishop Meerschaert speaks of visiting the place on his first pastoral tour in 1891. In 1912 Father William Hall, pastor of Coalgate, built a narrow frame structure, named St. David's. The small sacristy served also as a sleeping room when the priest came to hold services.

Father Peter Paul Schaeffer, who had earlier been director at St. Joseph's Orphanage near Bethany, was pastor, between 1930 and 1935, of a mission area centered in Tishomingo. The Depression era was also a time of social experiment. Father Schaeffer undertook to establish a Catholic colony in the Washita River valley southeast of Tishomingo. He met with some success in this, although it turned out to be temporary. The colony was located in the midst of an 8,000-acre cooperative known as the Washita Farms. Father Schaeffer built a somewhat larger church near the colony, which he called St. Anthony's. When plans were made in the late 1930's to build Lake Texoma, the Washita Farms development had to be moved. St. Anthony's church therefore was moved to the city of Tishomingo where it now stands, across the street from Murray State College.

For a time, Durant, a much larger town, was a mission of Tishomingo, but now Tishomingo and Madill (in neighboring Marshall County) are served by the pastor of Ardmore.

SULPHUR ◇ *St. Francis*

IN this summer resort town, with its salubrious sulphur spring, there was a small Catholic chapel as early as 1895. During the tourist season the priest from Ardmore would hold services there on some Sundays, later occasionally on weekdays, until finally he ceased coming altogether. The building, in need of repairs, was virtually abandoned.

After World War I the government built a veterans' hospital on the heights south of Sulphur. Father Eloi Justou, O.S.B., who had been a chaplain in France during the conflict, began visiting patients at the hospital. He also sought out Catholics in the general area. In 1923 a church was built with the help of Catholic Extension and dedicated to St. Anne. Benedictine monks from Sacred Heart Abbey attended the church, at first monthly and then, beginning around 1940, on a weekly basis.

It was World War II that gave fresh impetus to growth in Sulphur. In 1953 Bishop McGuinness instructed Father Alexander Andrews of Ardmore to prepare plans for a new church in Sulphur. This was done, and the bishop dedicated the completed structure on Palm Sunday, 1954. (Father Andrews died of cancer a few hours before the dedication ceremony took place.)

At the same time, Sulphur became a mission of the Ardmore parish. In 1966, Father Joseph Thompson was named associate pastor of St. Mary's, Ardmore, but with instructions to make his residence at Sulphur. The next year, after he had made the necessary preparations, St. Francis was named an independent parish, with Father Thompson as first resident pastor. Since 2002, however, Sulphur has assumed dependent status under the care of the pastor of Ada.

Seminole Nation

November 16, 1907

THE Seminole tribe originated within the Creek Nation, migrating into Florida from present-day Georgia around 1750; eventually this portion of the Creeks became known as Seminoles, a word meaning runaway. After the American War of Independence, Florida Indians made incursions on Georgia settlements, leading Andrew Jackson to fight the First Seminole War in 1817-18. By the Adams-Onis Treaty of 1821, Spain ceded Florida to the United States, opening the way for white settlement in Florida. The government came under pressure to remove the Seminoles, and so in 1832 the Treaty of Payne's Landing provided that the tribe would move to the Indian Territory. Removals began in 1836, but opposition to the government led to the Second Seminole War, which lasted from 1835 to 1842. Using guerilla tactics, several hundred Seminoles retreated into the Everglades and successfully frustrated American plans to remove them. About 3,700 Seminoles came to Oklahoma under military escort. Their reservation today is coterminous with Seminole County. By the time of the Civil War, the Oklahoma Seminoles had been extensively evangelized by Baptist and Presbyterian missionaries.

Nov. 16 1907

Seminole

MAUD
St. Cecilia

THE small town of Maud, located near the border of Seminole and Pottawatomie Counties, became a Catholic mission in 1955 as a result of the work of Father Thomas Rabideau, O.S.B., pastor of Seminole. Father Thomas' term as pastor was rather lengthy— from January 1951 to December 1996, a total of 46 years.

SEMINOLE
Immaculate Conception

ALTHOUGH oil exploration began near Wewoka as early as 1902, it was not until 1923 and the discovery of the Greater Seminole Oil Field that the Seminole region experienced an economic boom. By September 1929, this had become the premier high-gravity oil field in the United States. The large influx of oilmen, a number of them Catholics, pointed to the need for a Catholic church in Seminole.

Catholics in Seminole County generally attended Mass in Shawnee or Holdenville until 1928, when Father Patrick McNamee, O.S.B., was placed in charge of the growing congregation and managed to put up a combination frame building to serve as a temporary place of worship and as a rectory, at 405 North First Street.

Father Martin Mulcahy, O.S.B., built a second church in 1938, Father Eloi Justou, O.S.B., erected a third at the original location in 1949. Finally, in 1963 Father Thomas Rabideau built the present church that stands on Highway 9. It was used for the first time at the Easter Vigil that year. The Seminole parish has always been under the care of the Benedictines of St. Gregory's Abbey.

WEWOKA
St. Joseph

THIS parish developed in 1948 as a project of Father Maurus Fuerstenberg, O.S.B., pastor of Holdenville in Hughes County, and a building committee of Wewoka Catholics. Father Maurus offered the first Mass in the new church on August 8, 1948. When the diocese of Tulsa was established in 1973, the boundary line ran between Seminole County and neighboring Hughes County. This created an awkward situation for the Catholics of Wewoka, for even though they remained in the archdiocese, their pastor resided at Holdenville, which now lay within the new diocese. It took some 25 years to straighten out the situation, but now Wewoka is a mission of Seminole.

Index of Places